MUTTable

Book Three

by Ashli D Wells

@ashlidcartoondogs on Instagram

Dedicated to God, Po, Thud, Princess, and Mopsy.

MUTTable=mutt+lovable

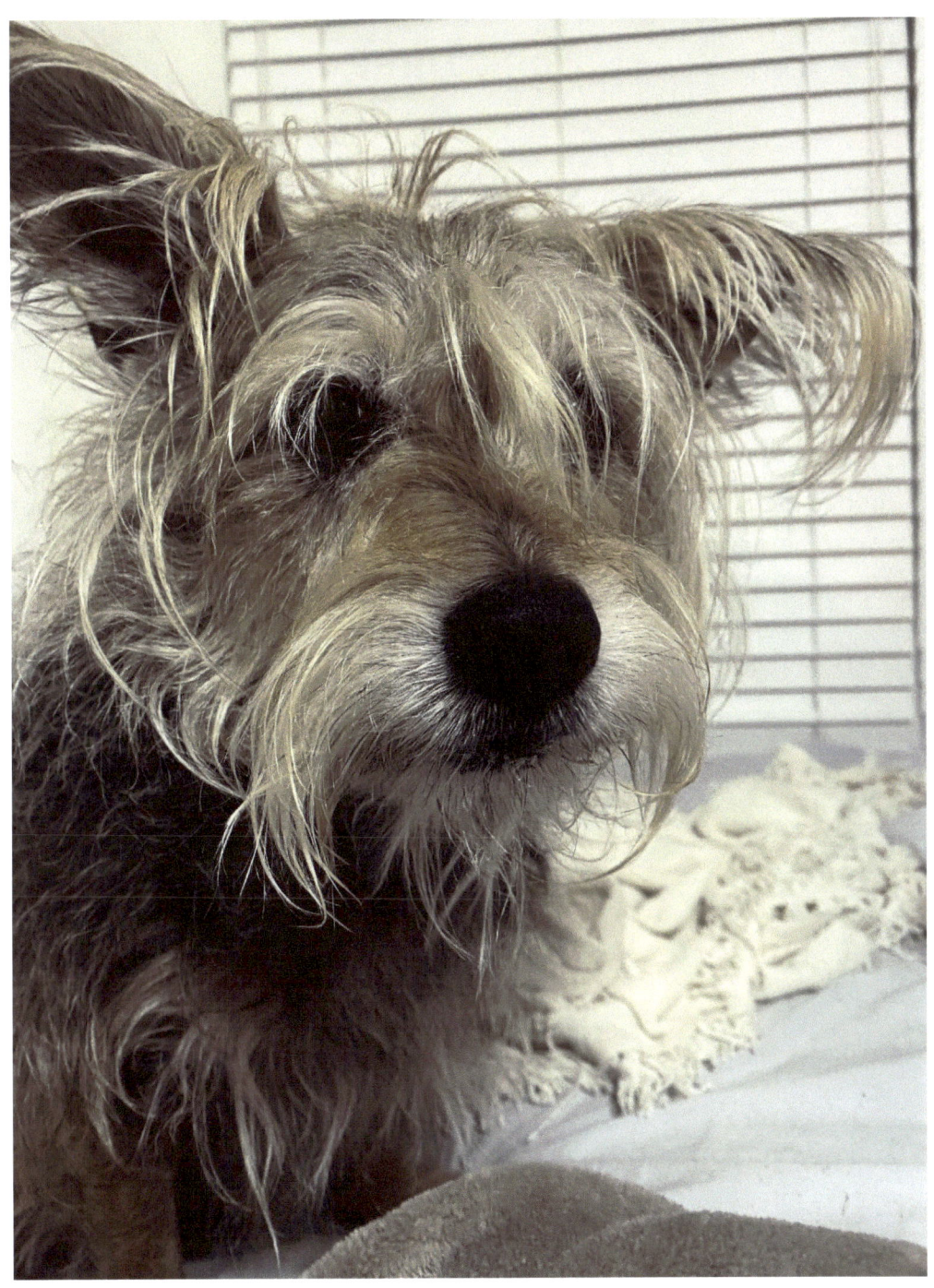

R.I.P. Jack Jack

MUTTable

Book Three

This MUTTable spans the years from 2021 till now. I have gone through several challenges over the last few years, but I am exceedingly happy to be back at what I do. Throughout the most difficult of times, a pleasant constant in my life has been, and will always be, the presence of dogs. I feel privileged to be able to capture their essence in my sculptures. I pray that my work exemplifies the joy and love that dogs bring to our lives. Making tiny dogs brings me immense joy, and I pray this MUTTable brings you joy. I absolutely love what I do.

MUTTable books are a combination of my commissioned work and dogs that I choose at random. I can be messaged directly on Instagram at https://www.instagram.com/ashlidcartoondogs. Thank you, Ashli D.

The Chair

by Ashli D Wells

I think you stole my chair, where my butt is supposed to sit.

You look so very comfy; I'll admit it's a perfect fit.

I really hate to ask you to vacate your chosen spot,

but I've been working all day, and it's my spot you got.

Don't look at me like that, without an ounce of guilt.

You have your own doggy bed, and even your own quilt.

You have all kinds of stuff that is your very own.

So, all I really want is my chair when I get home.

I've been on my feet all day, and I need to take a rest.

I know my favorite seat is the spot that you like best.

It seems that moving along is not a choice you'll choose.

So, maybe we just compromise, then neither has to lose.

If I can just sit down in the place that you want to be,

then I can sit in the chair, and you can sit on me.

Doggies

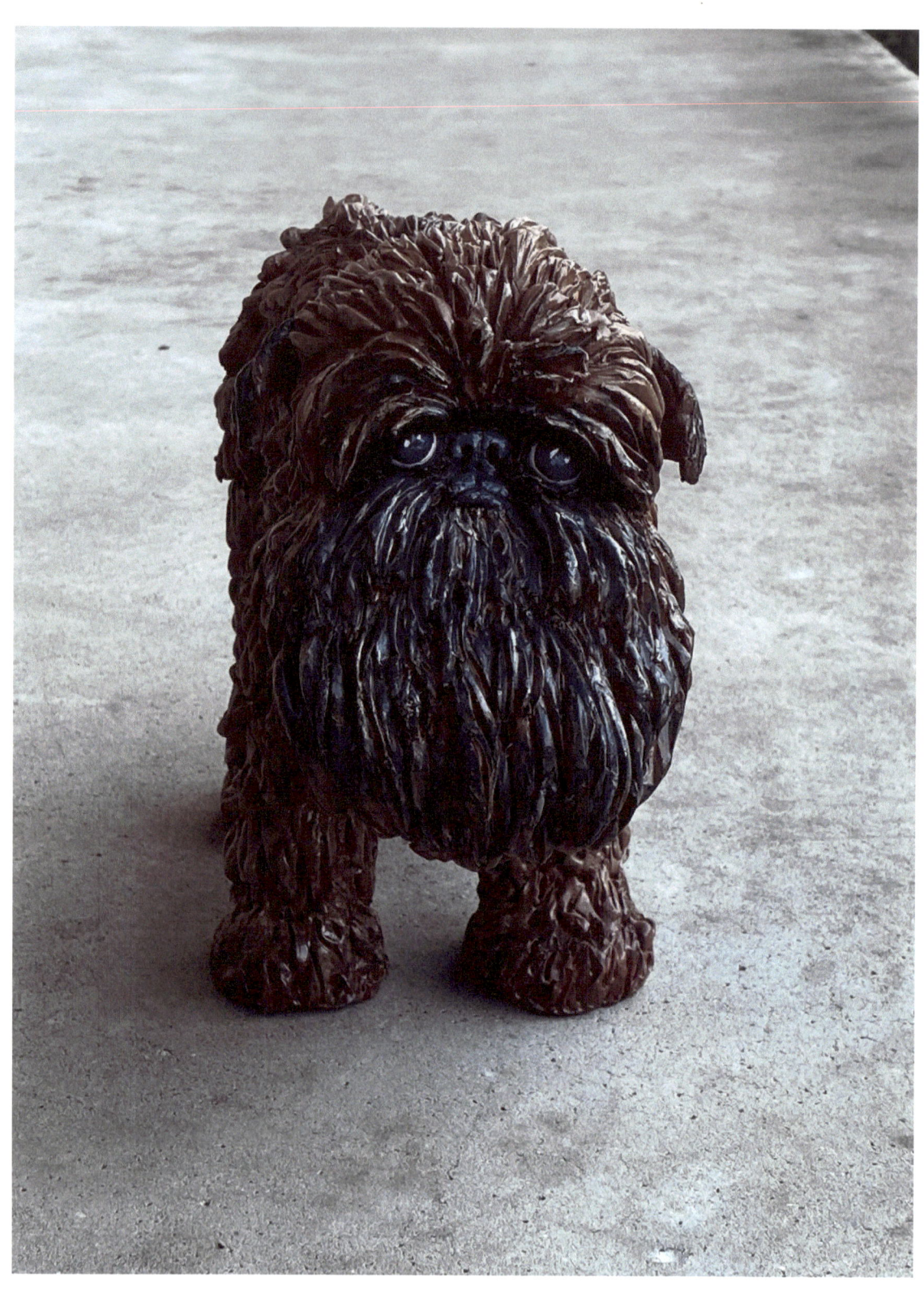

Ralphie @ralphienyc

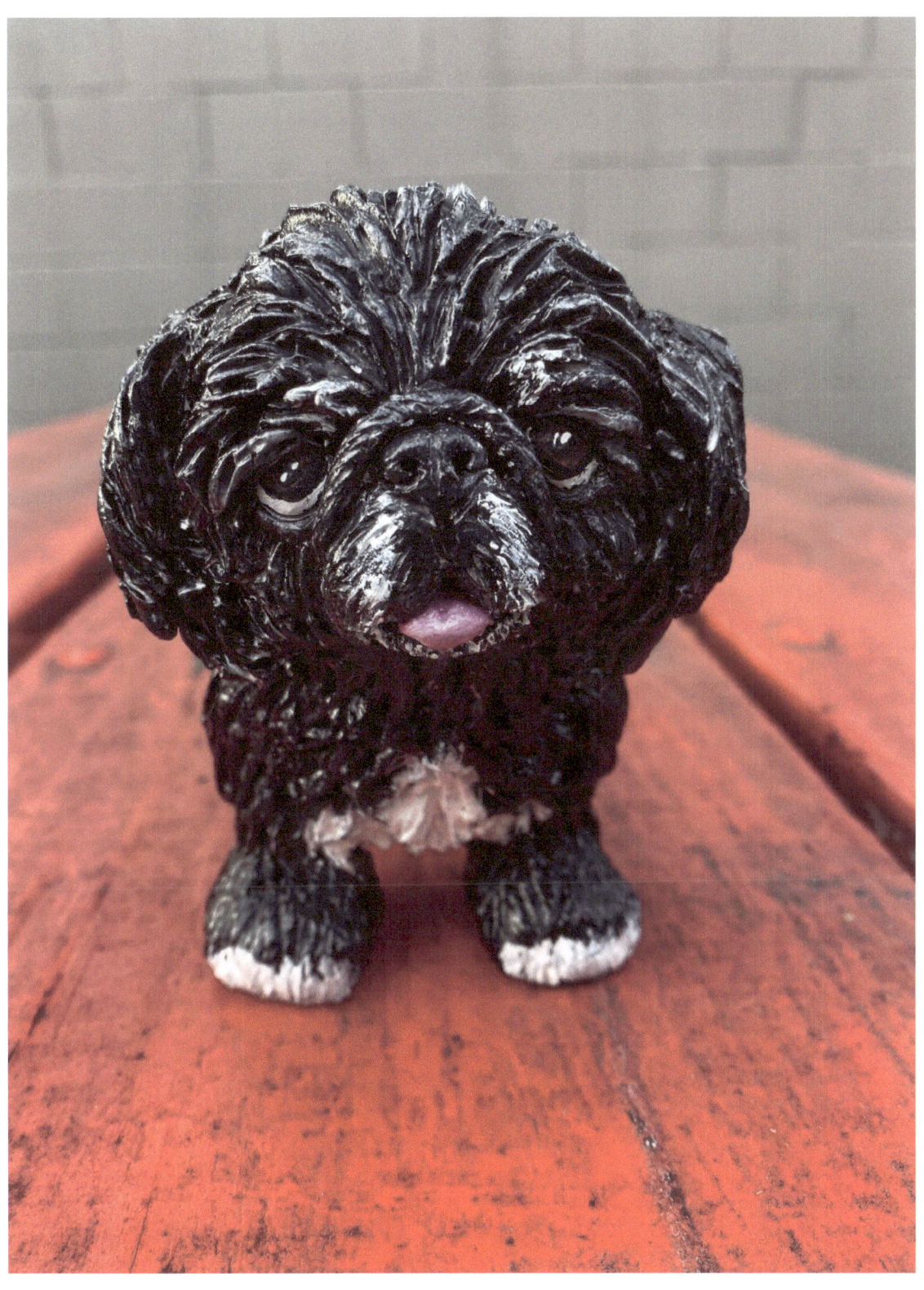

Ollie @sirolivierlaurence

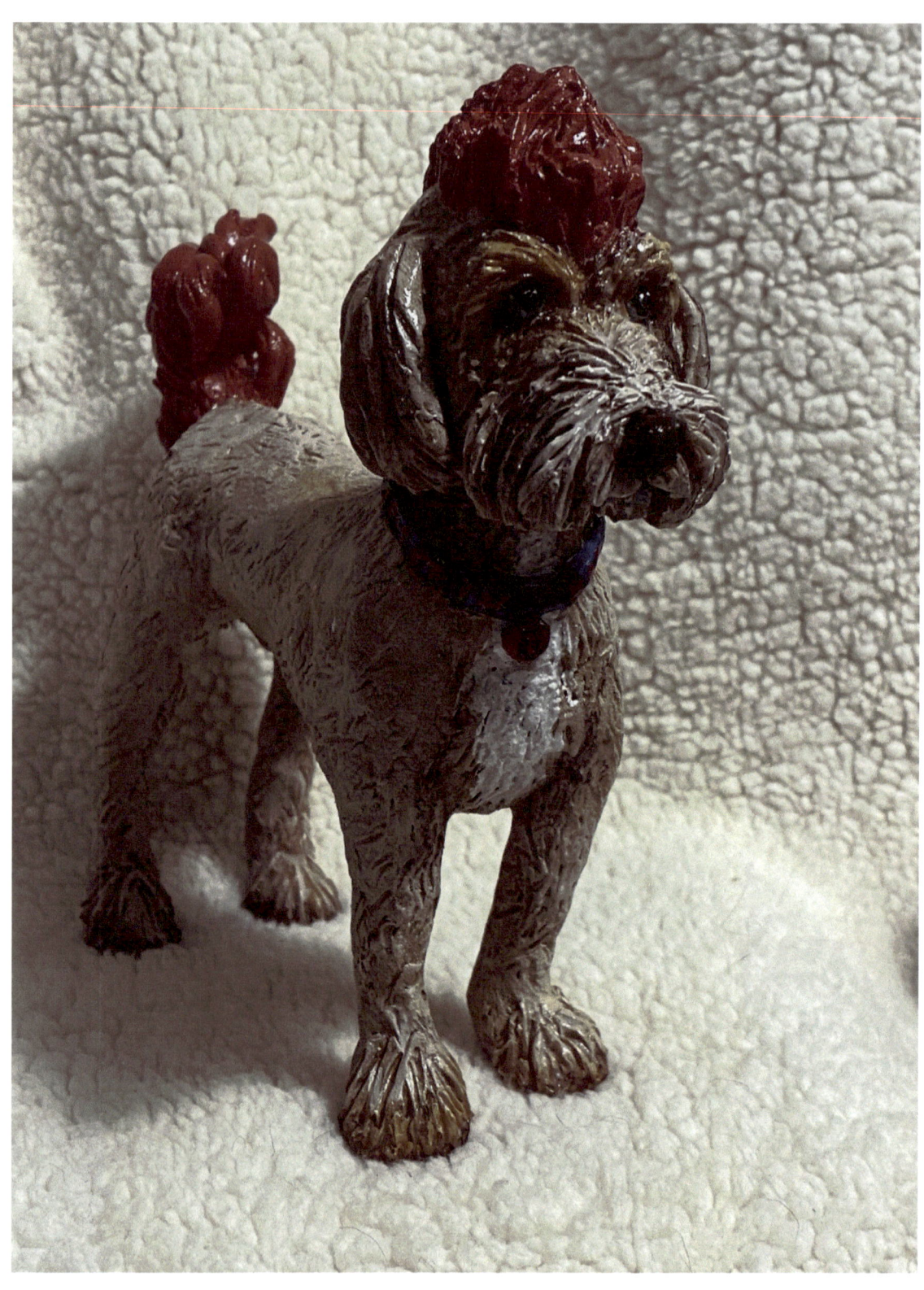

Breckin @breckindoodle.17

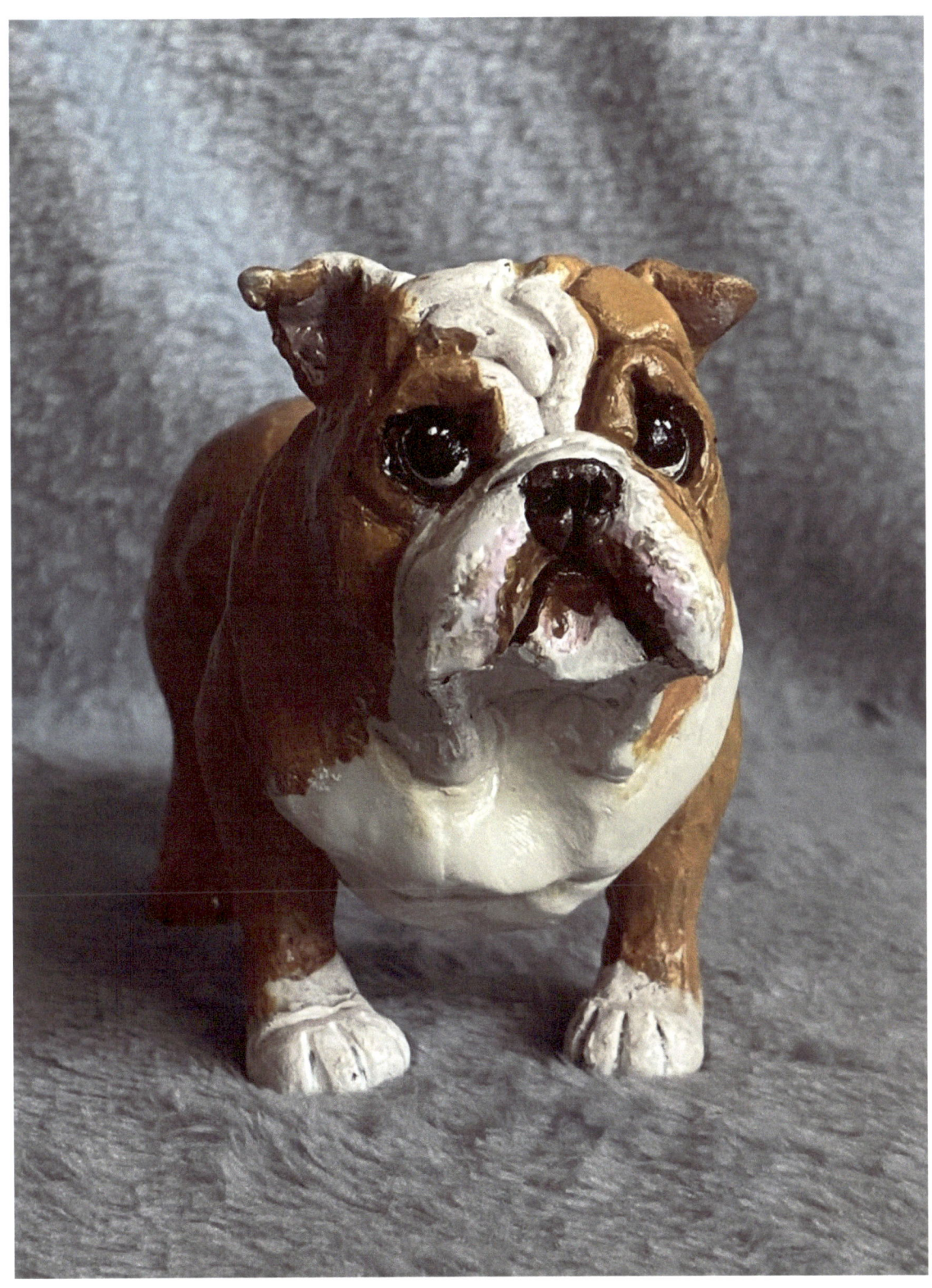

Wilhemina

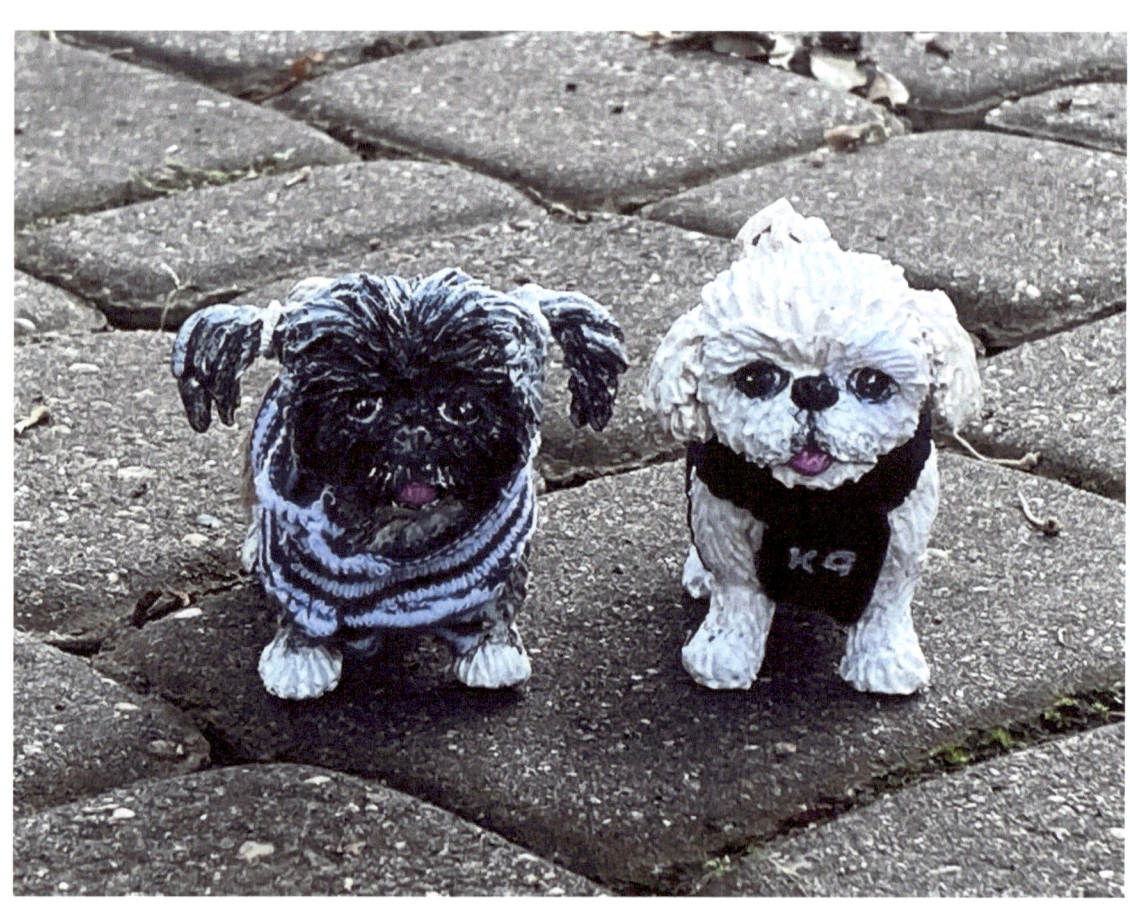

Pepper and Cloud @powerfluff

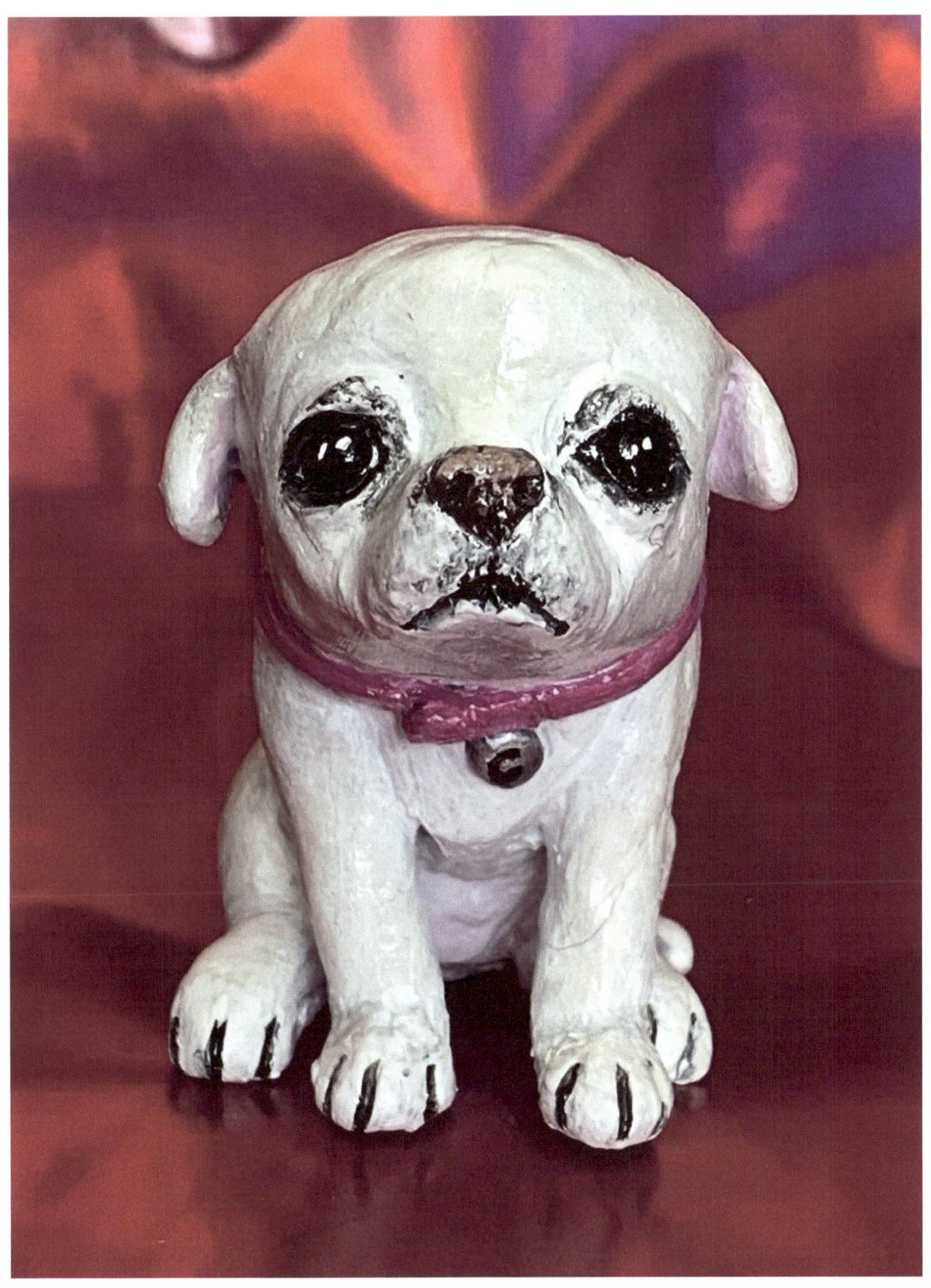

Cheena

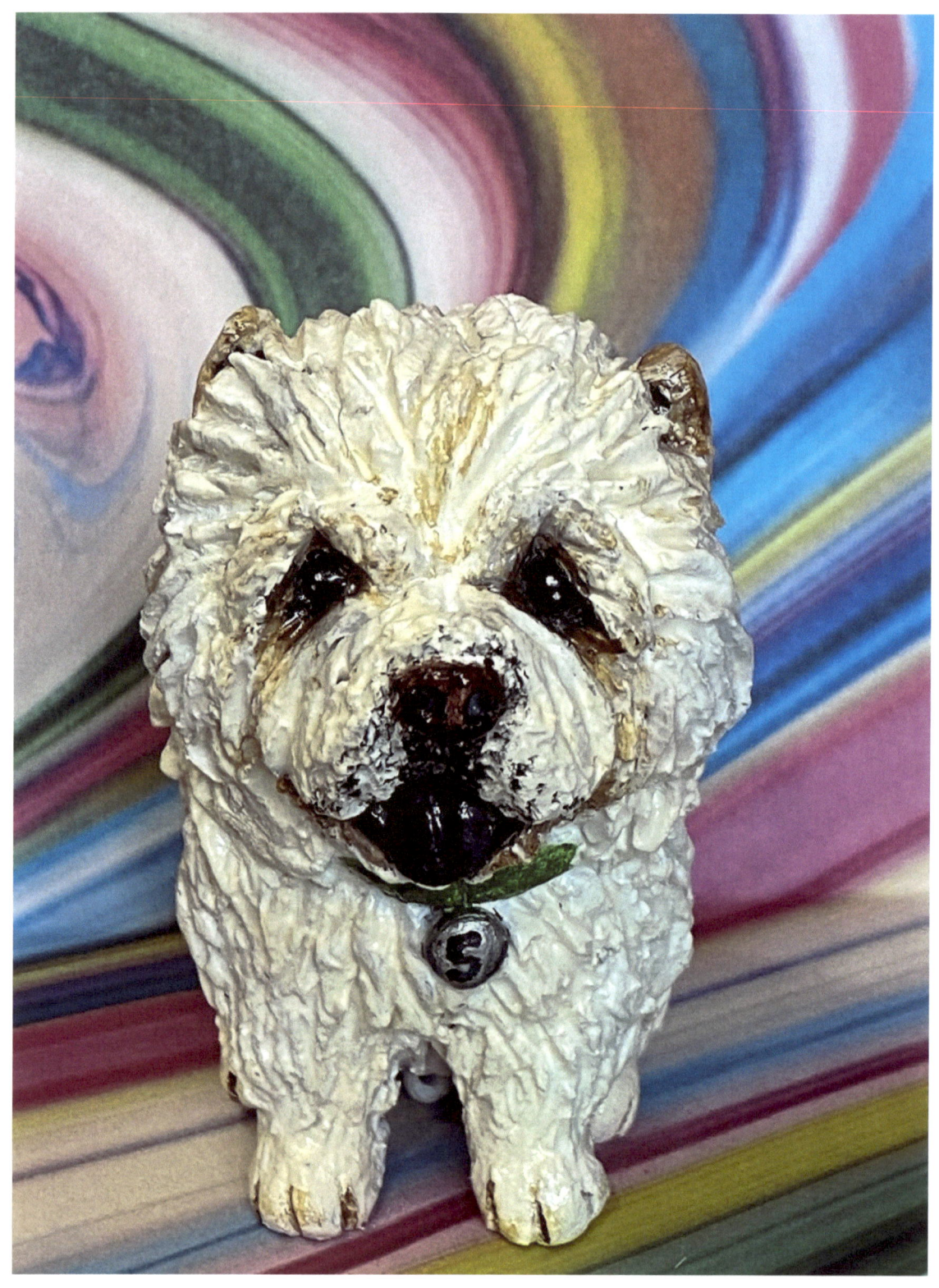

Safar

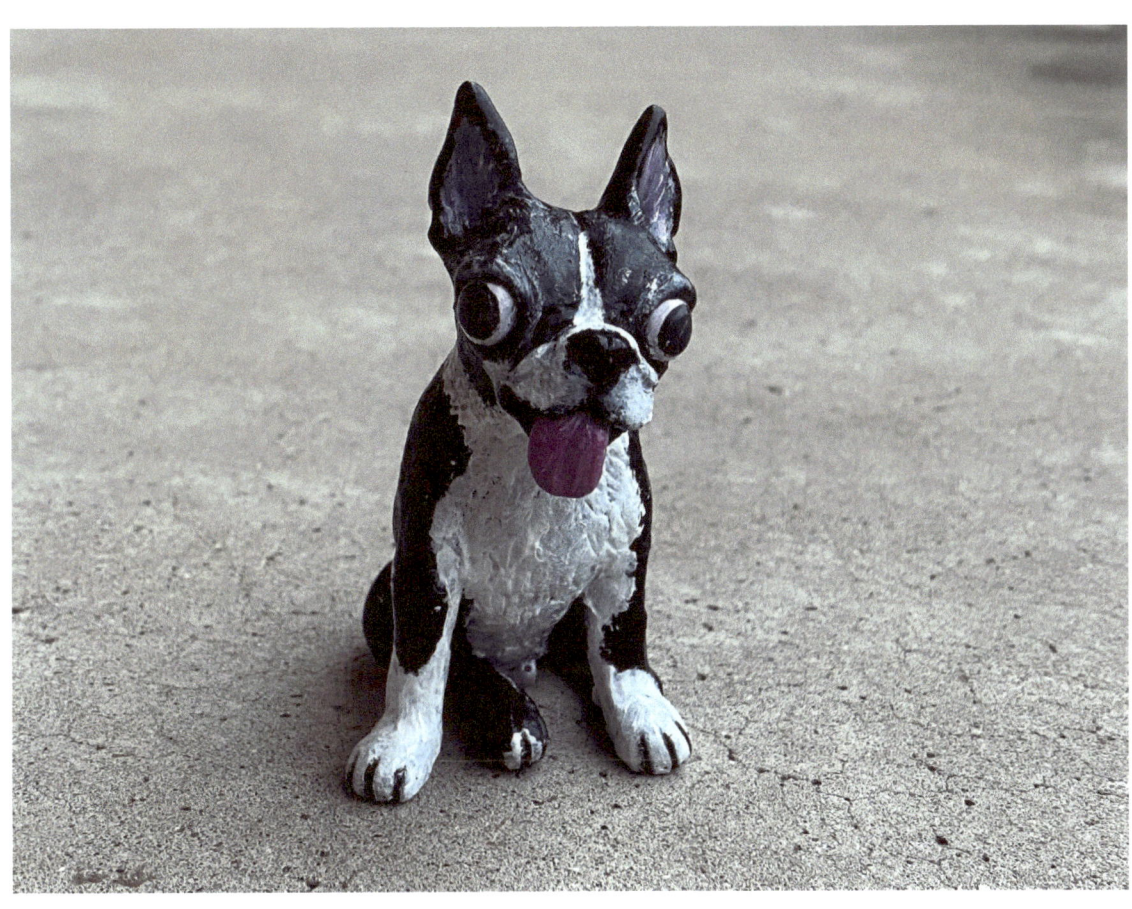

Buster @mrbusterbust and @thehoppyhound

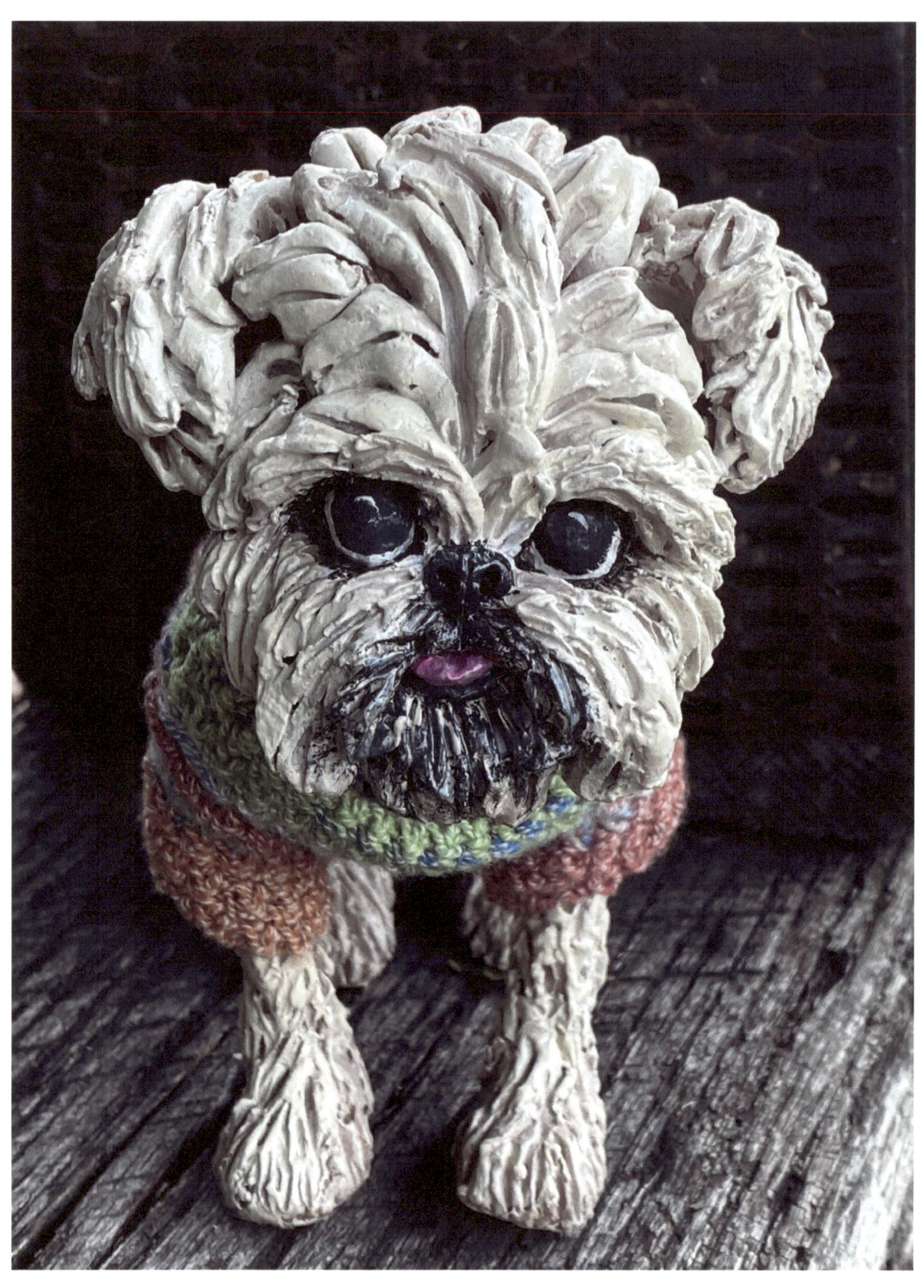

Molly @timeformolly

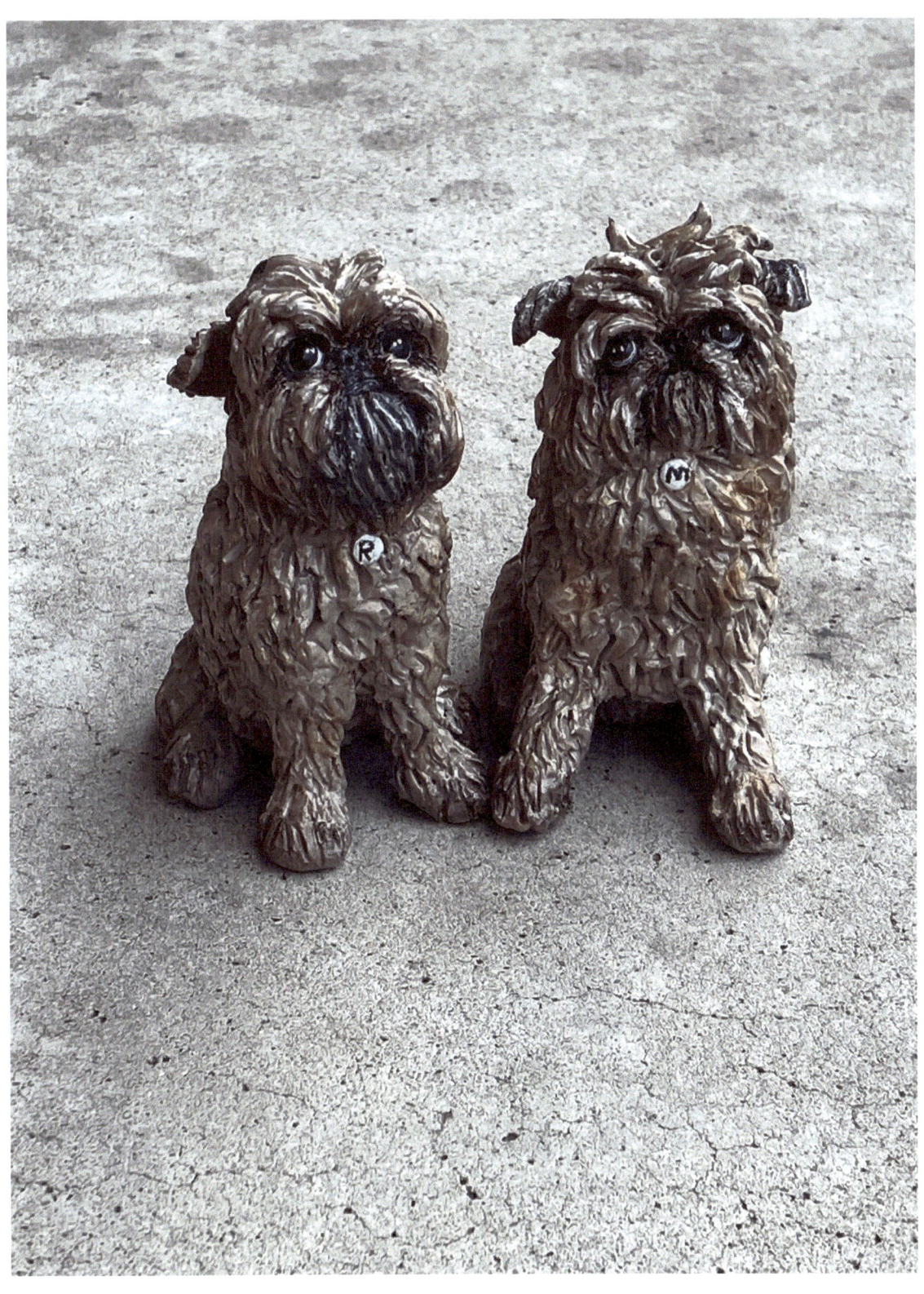

Rudy and Machie @rudyandmachie

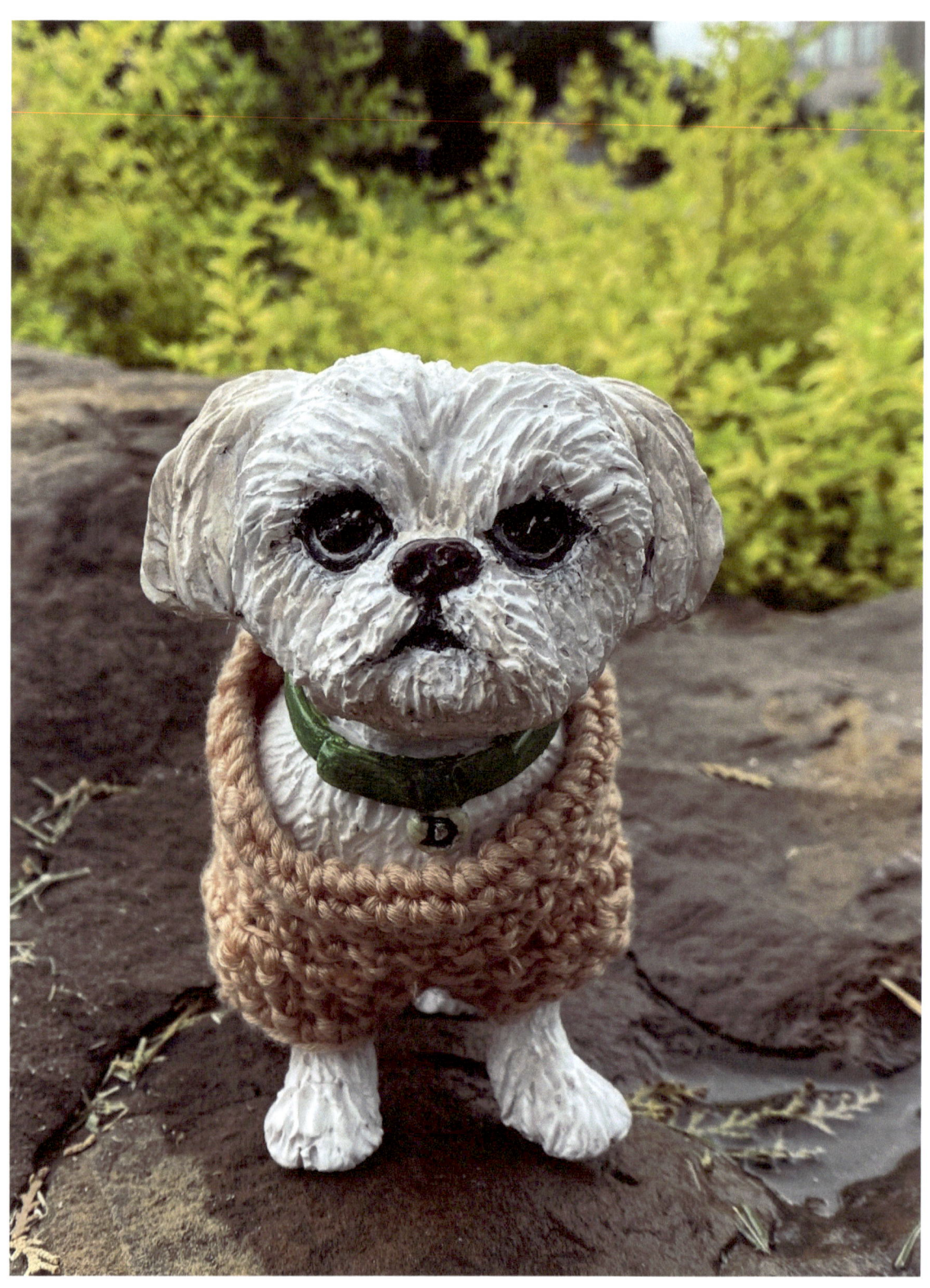

Dino @dinothedisableddog

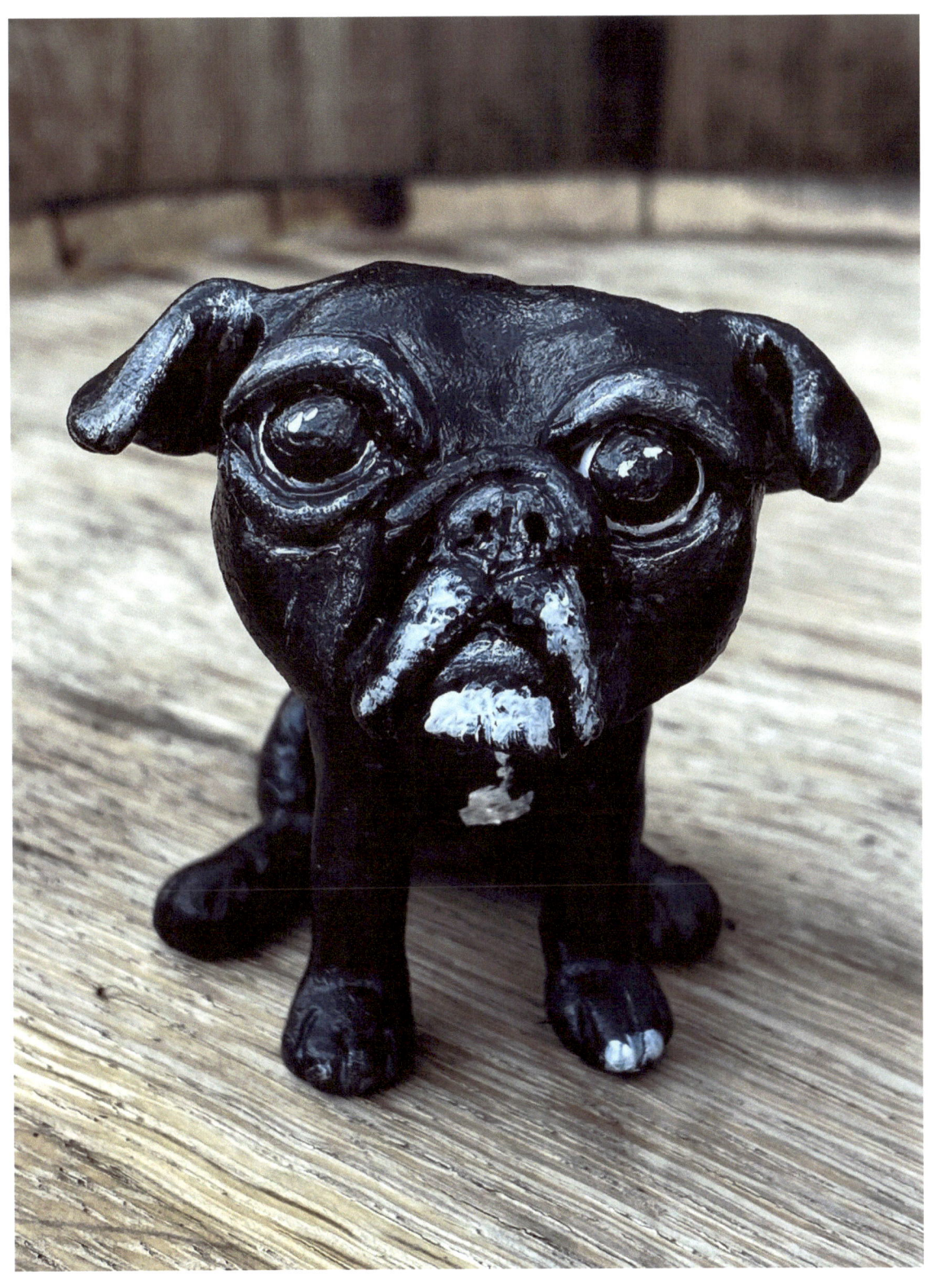

Bijou @bijouthepugzu

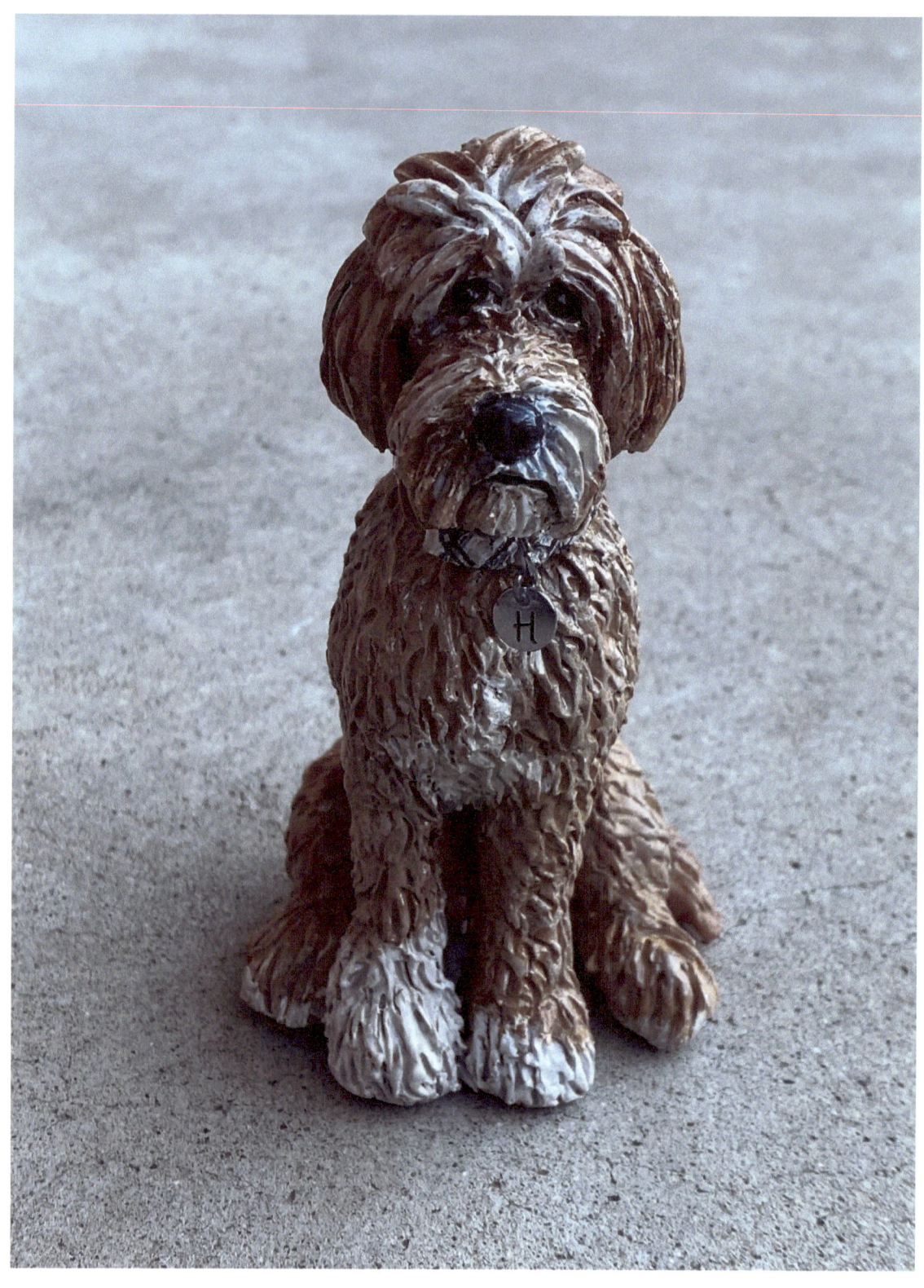

Hudson @logan_hudson_doodleduo

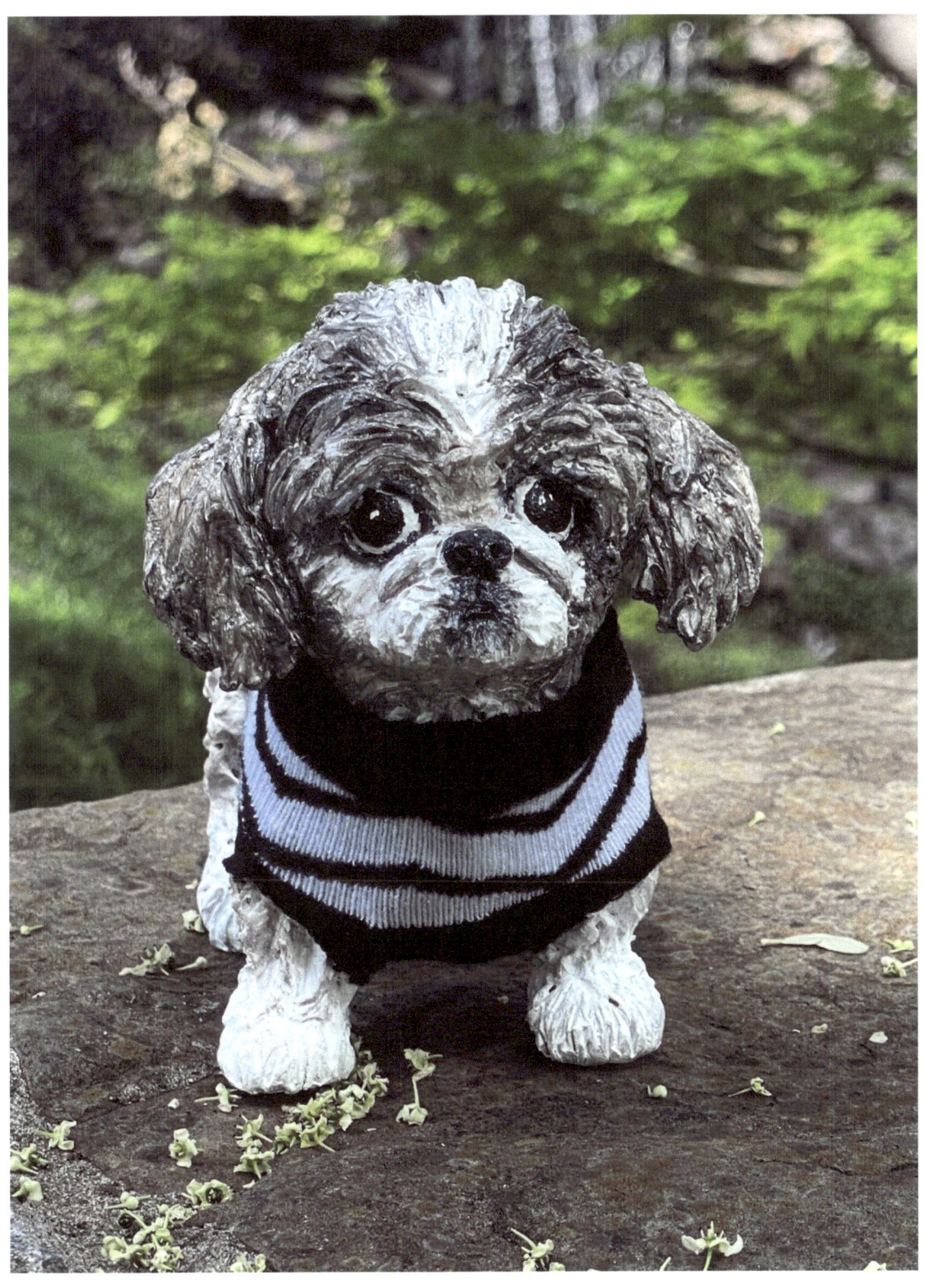

Fuzz Aldrin @chuganese

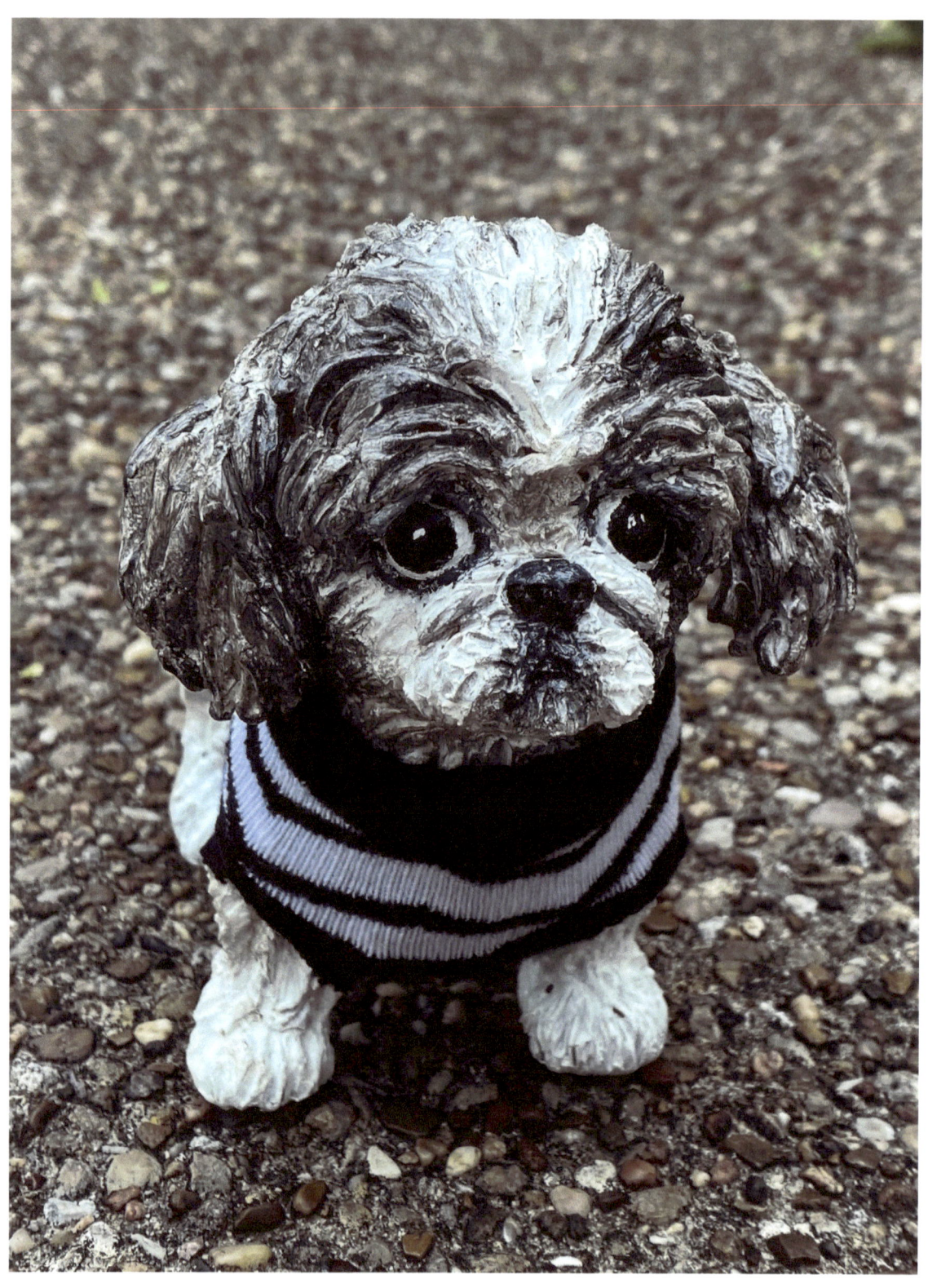

Fuzz Aldrin @chuganese

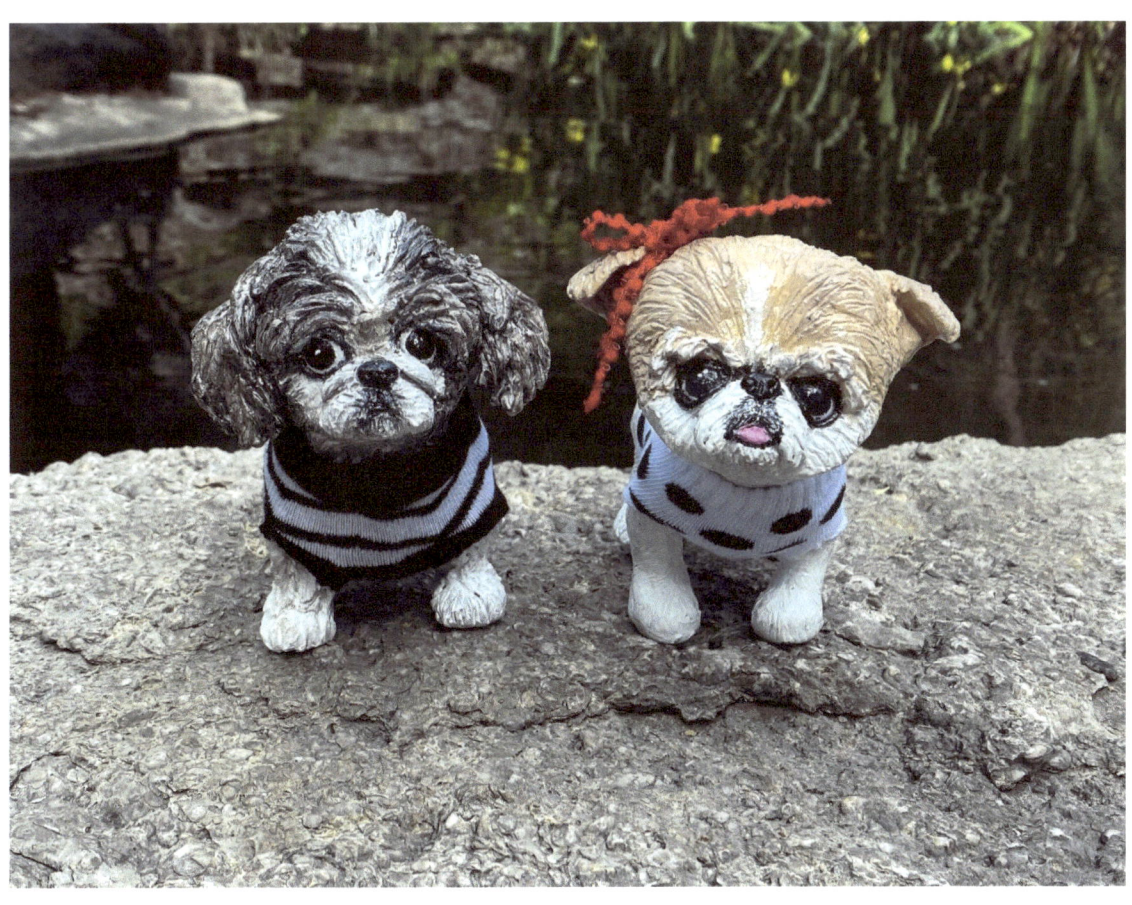

Fuzz Aldrin @chuganese and Cookie @itmecookie__

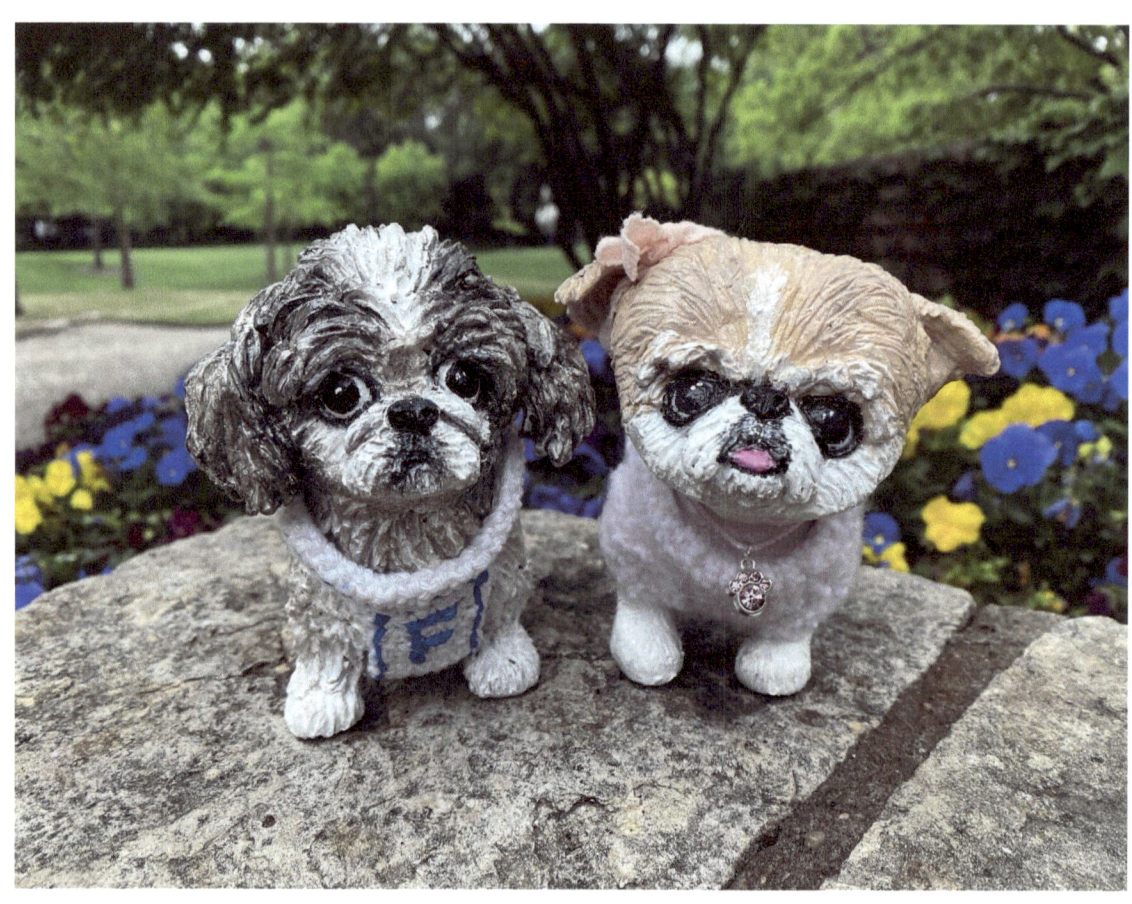

Fuzz Aldrin @chuganese and Cookie @itmecookie__

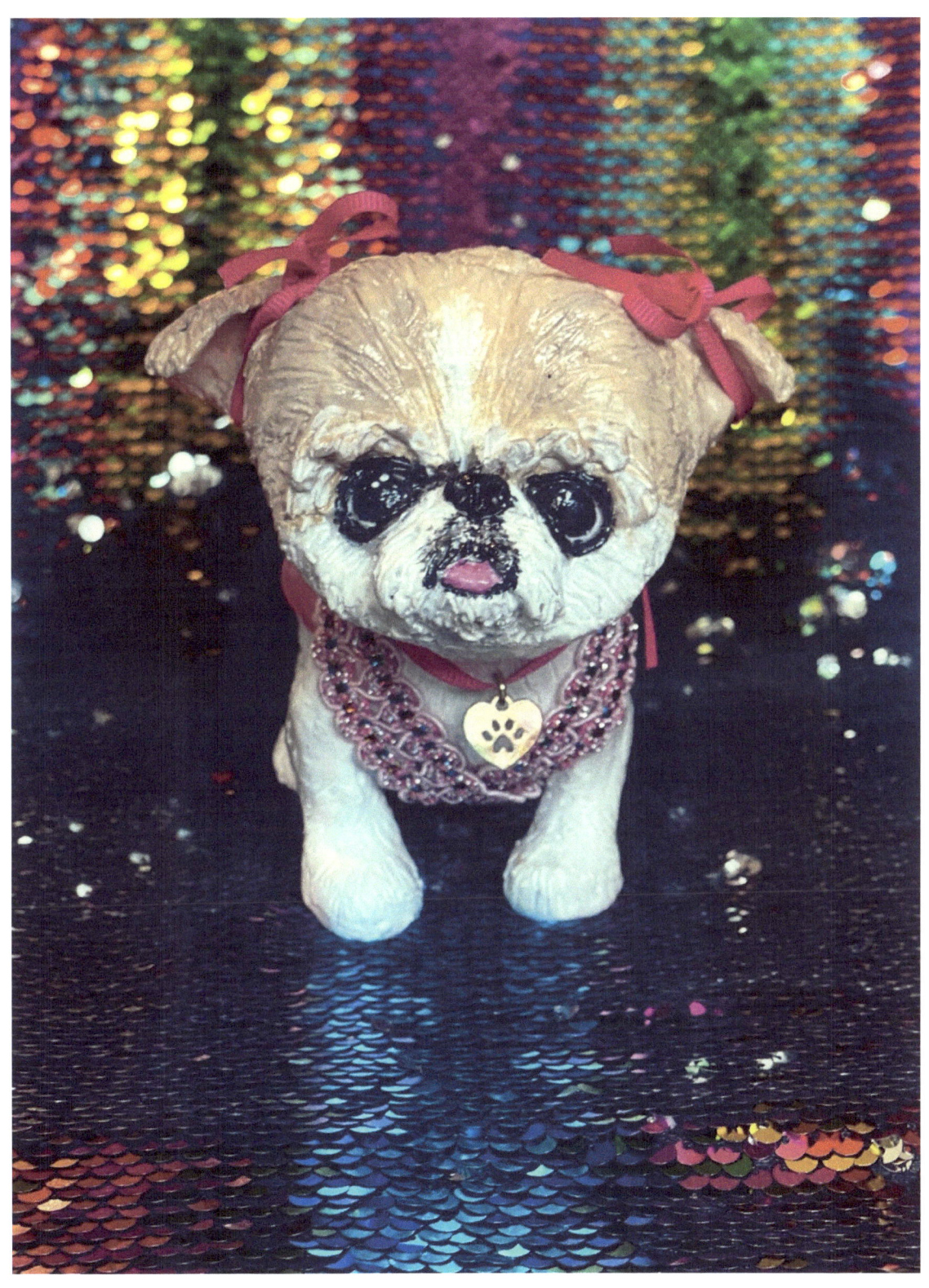

Cookie @itmecookie__

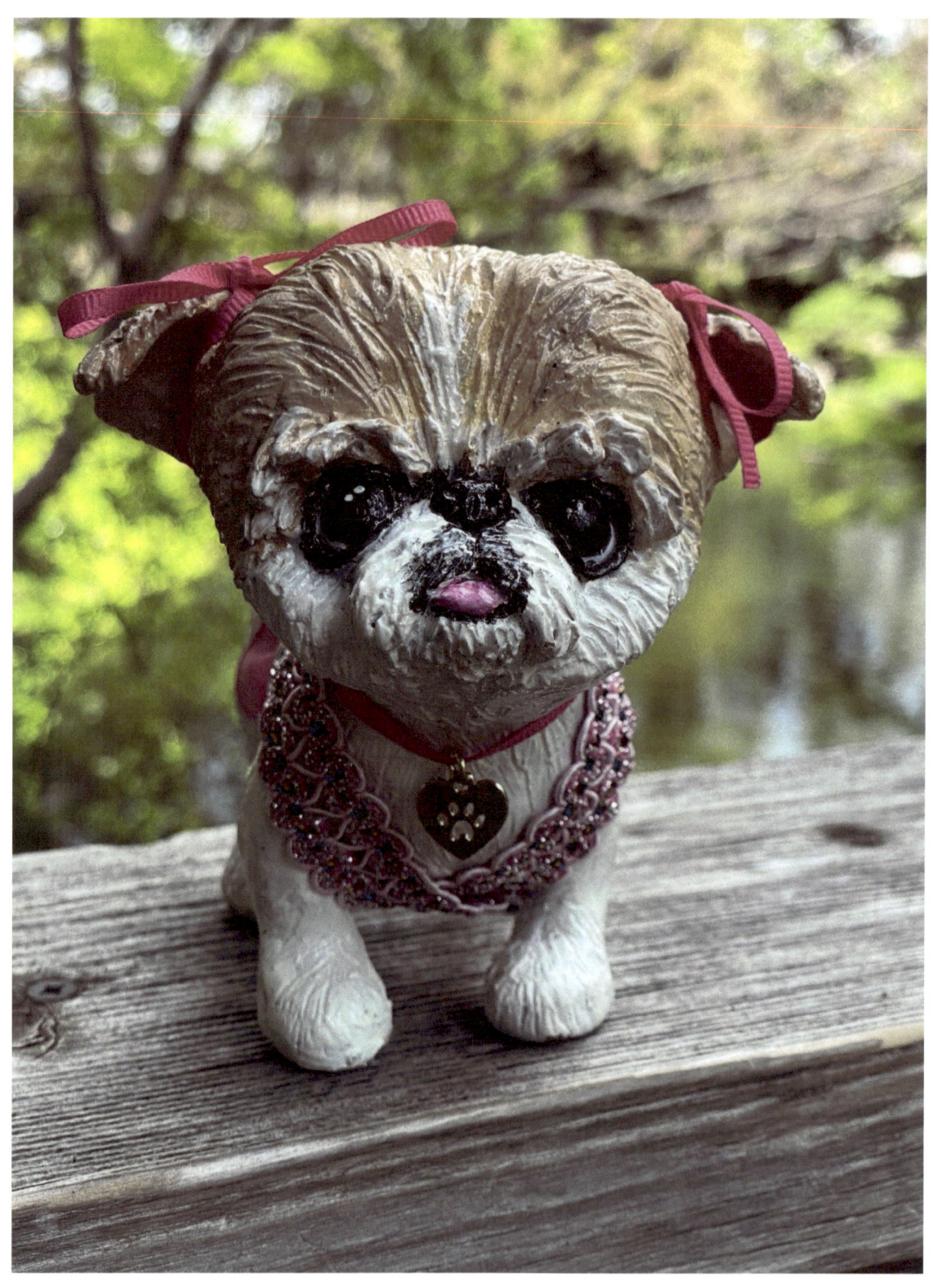

Cookie @itmecookie__

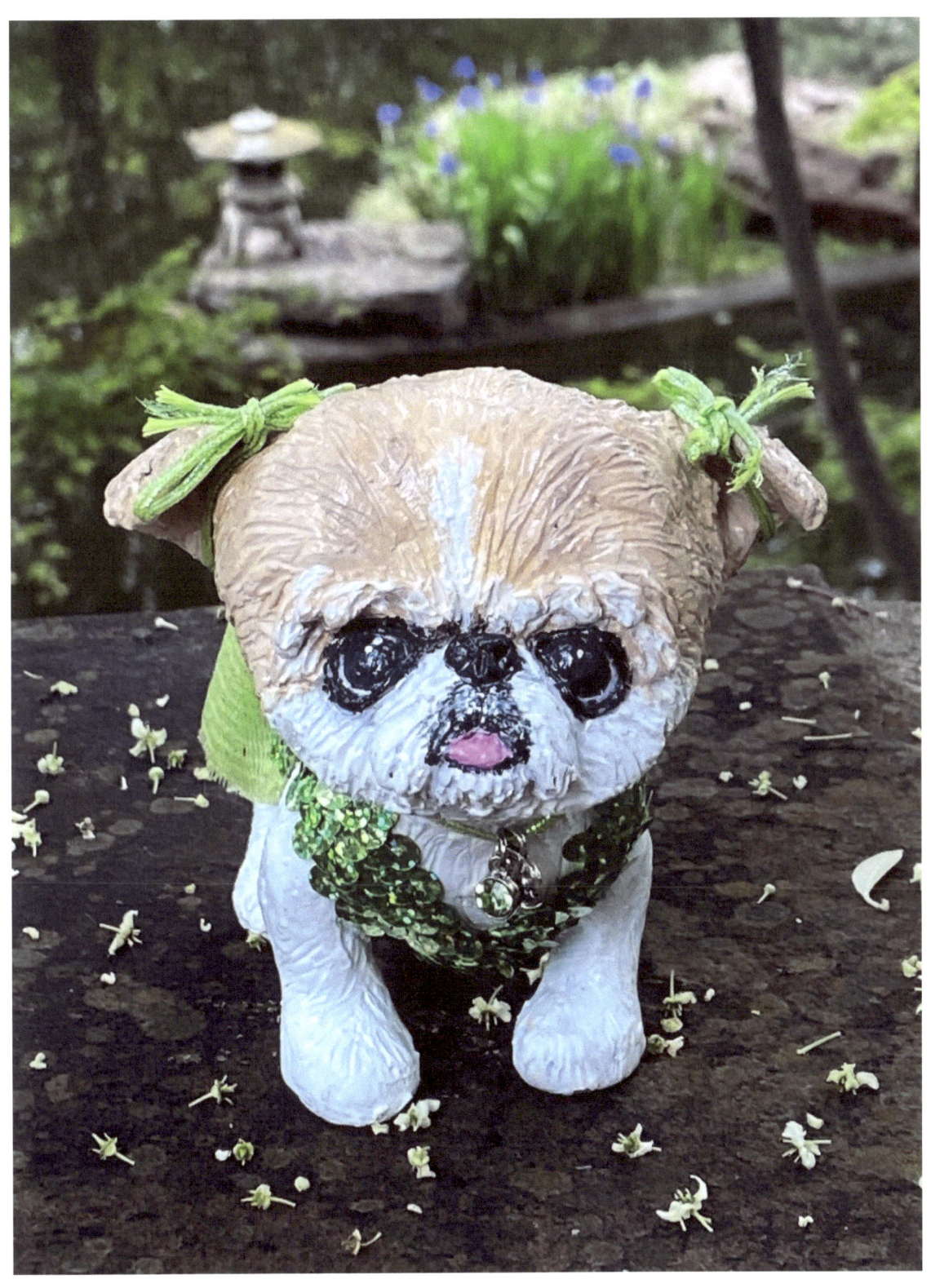

Cookie @itmecookie__

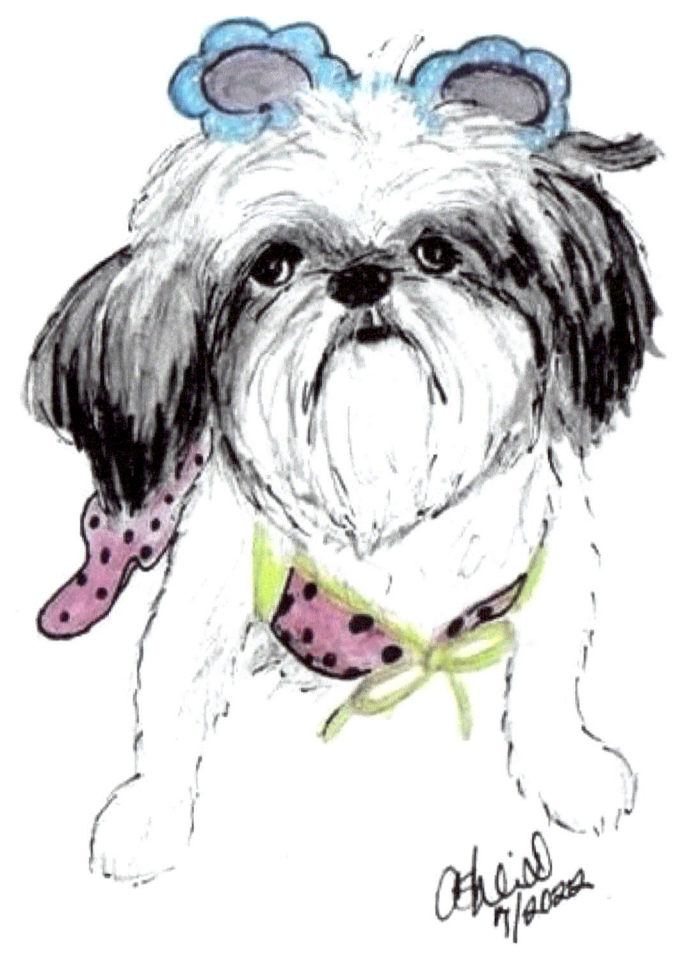

Scarlett @scarlettsfaith

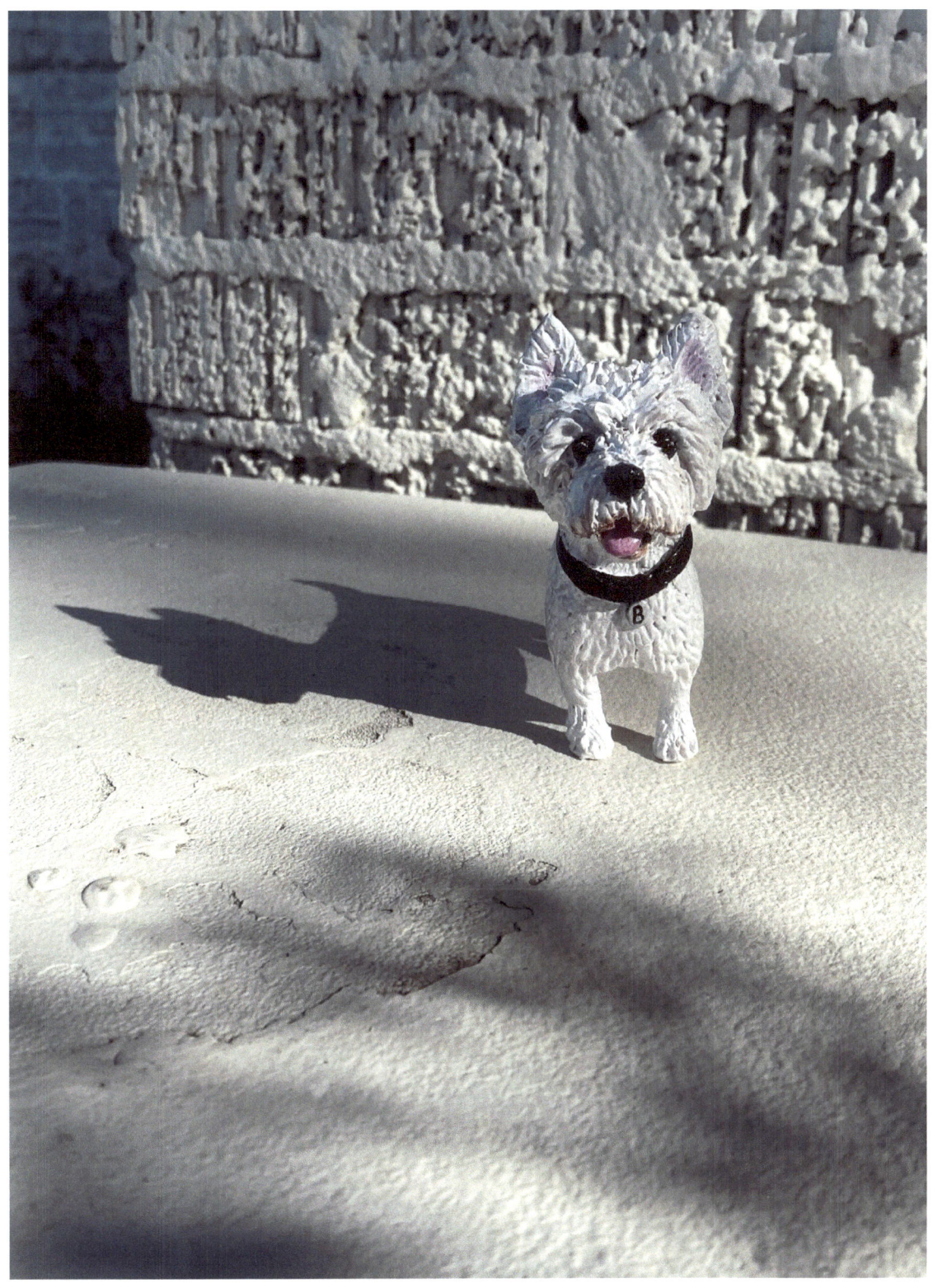

Bodie

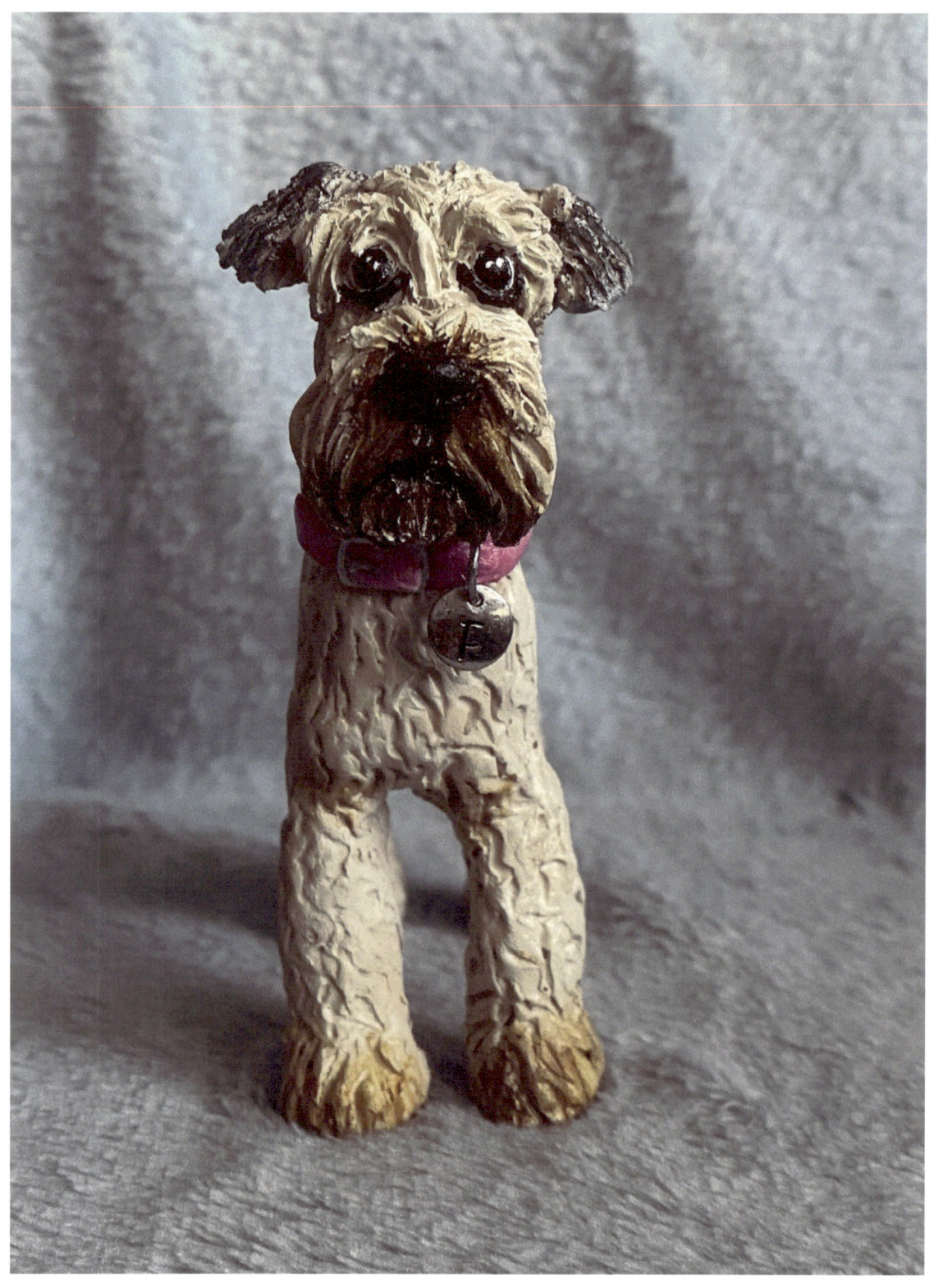

Fennie

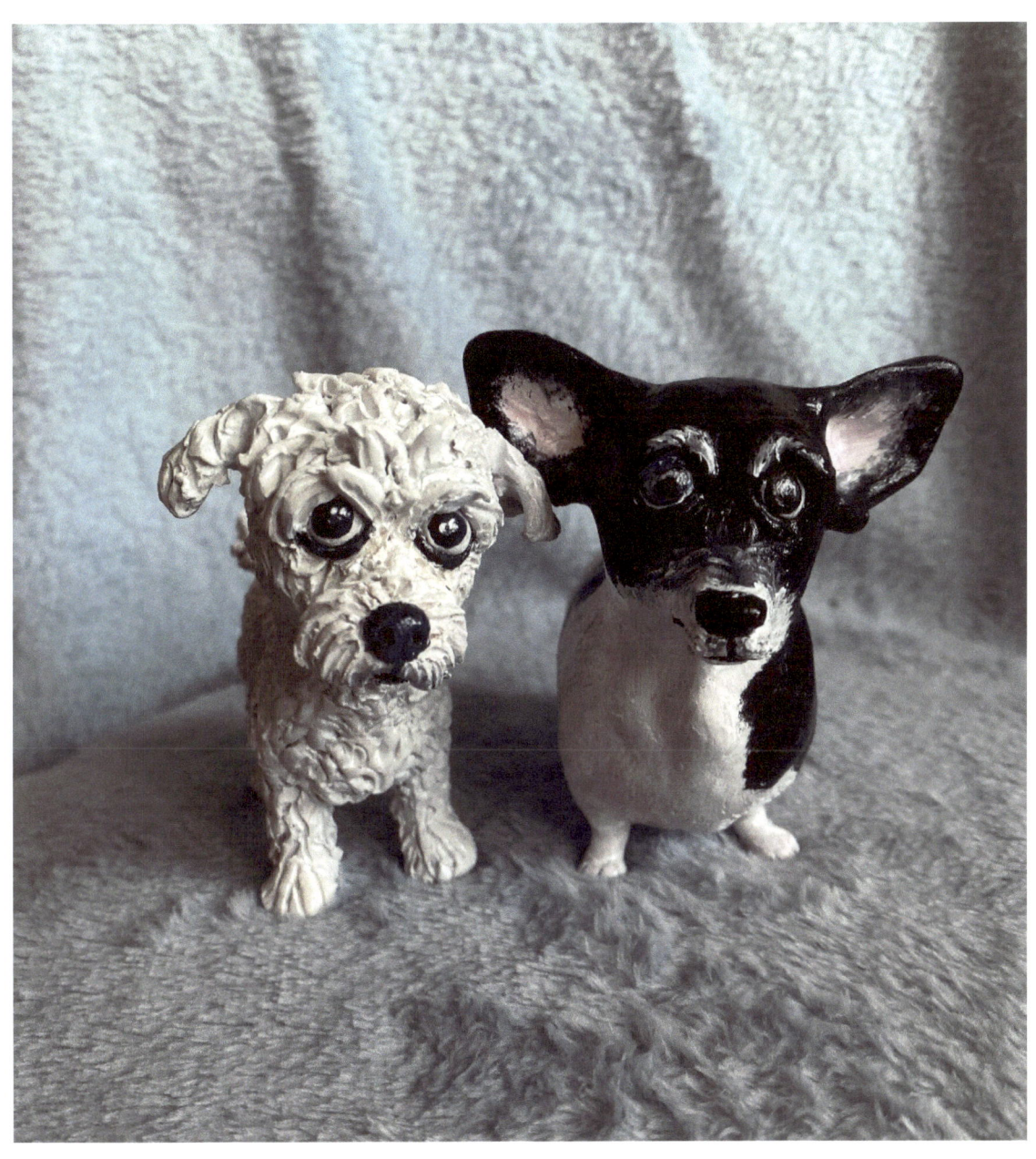

Annabelle and Woody (former shelter residents) @fortworthacc

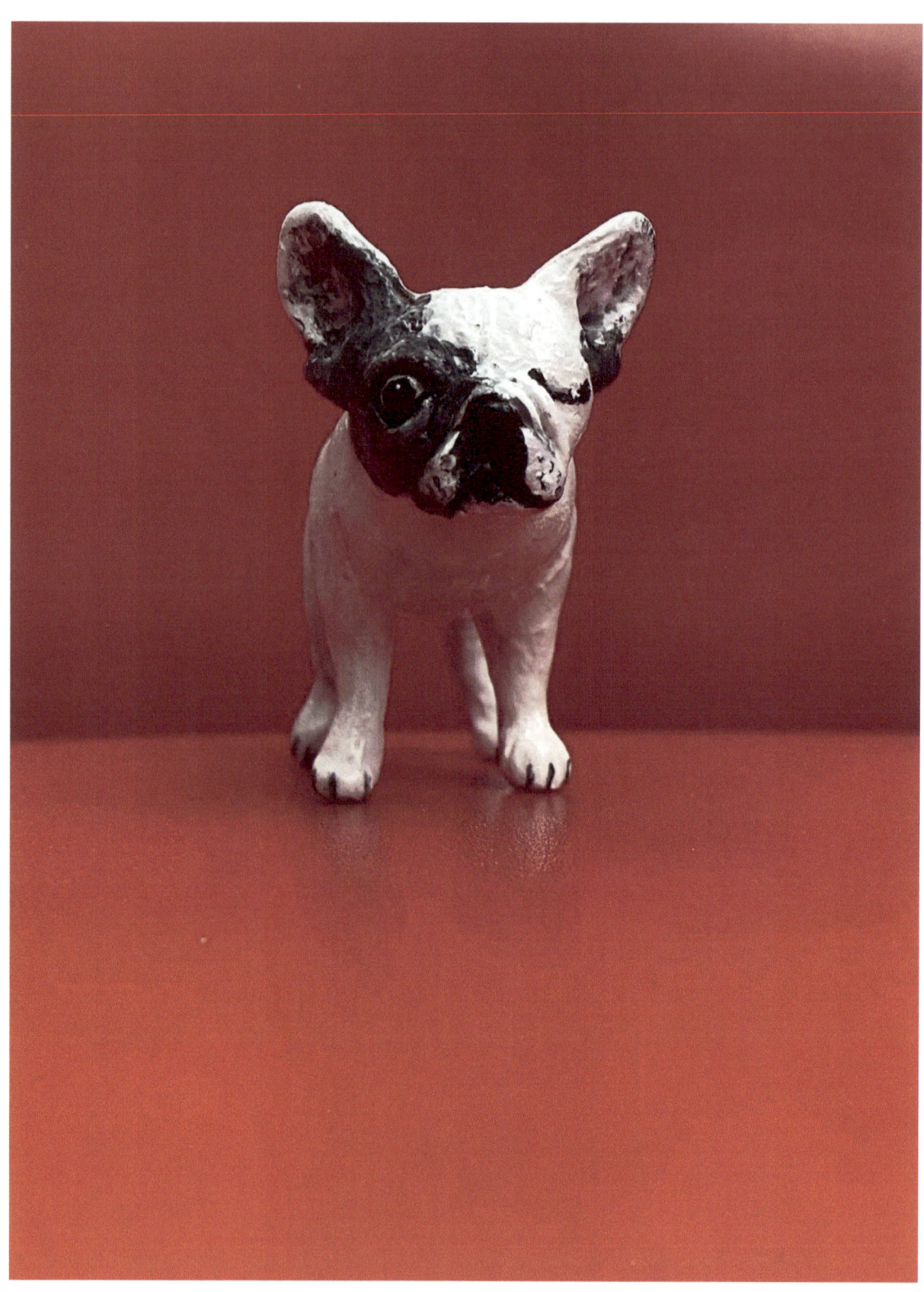

Tink @theo_and_tiny_tink

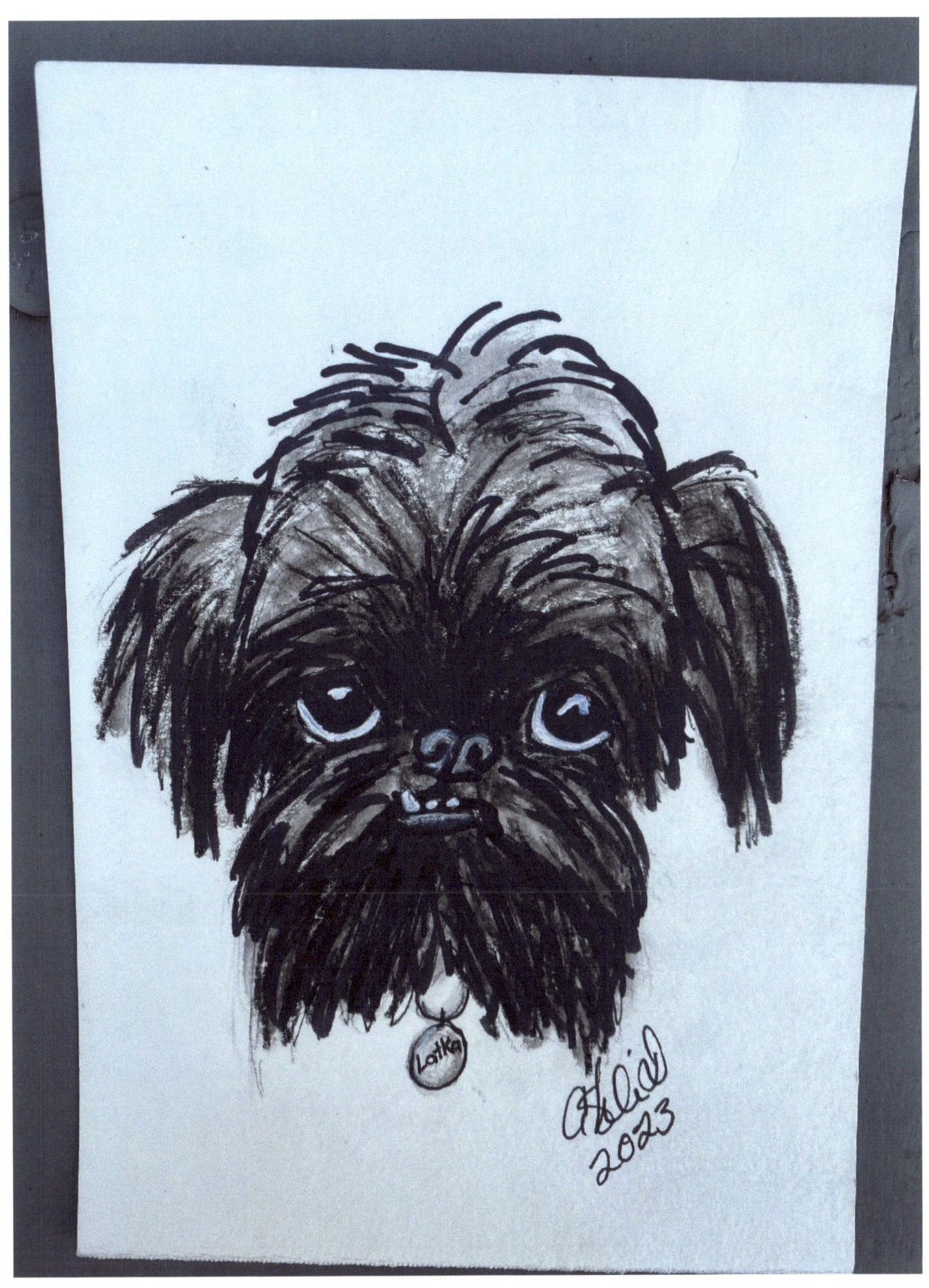

Latka @latka_and_beans

Weenita Wags

by Ashli D Wells

She's rough around the edges and made of paper mâché,
but Weenita's sole purpose is to make you smile today.

She isn't quite real, just a product of pretend:
a giant weenie dog who wants to be your friend.

So, keep your eye out for Weenita in case she strolls by,
and don't be too shy to tell Weenita, "Hi."

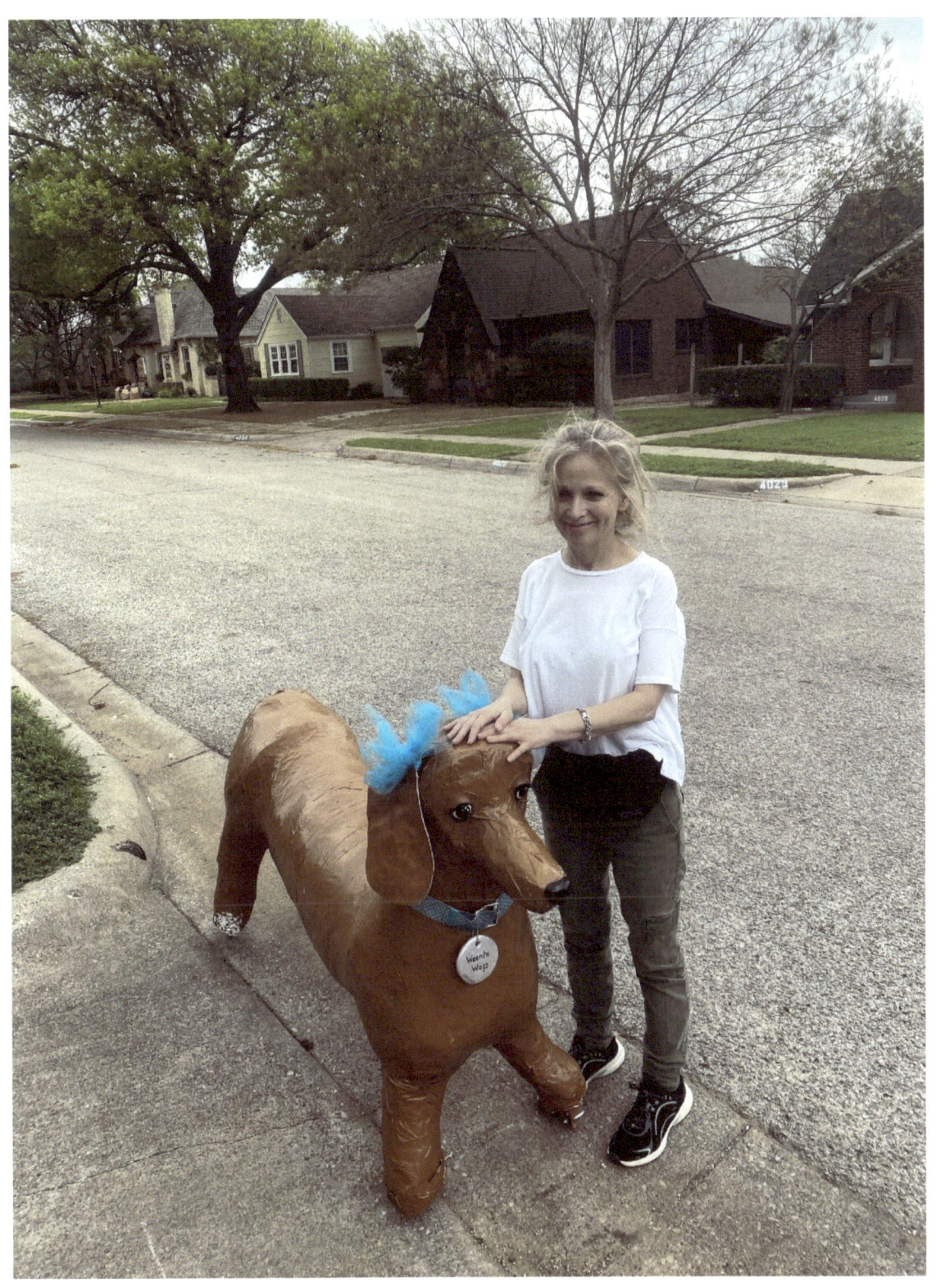

Weenita Wags and Ashli D

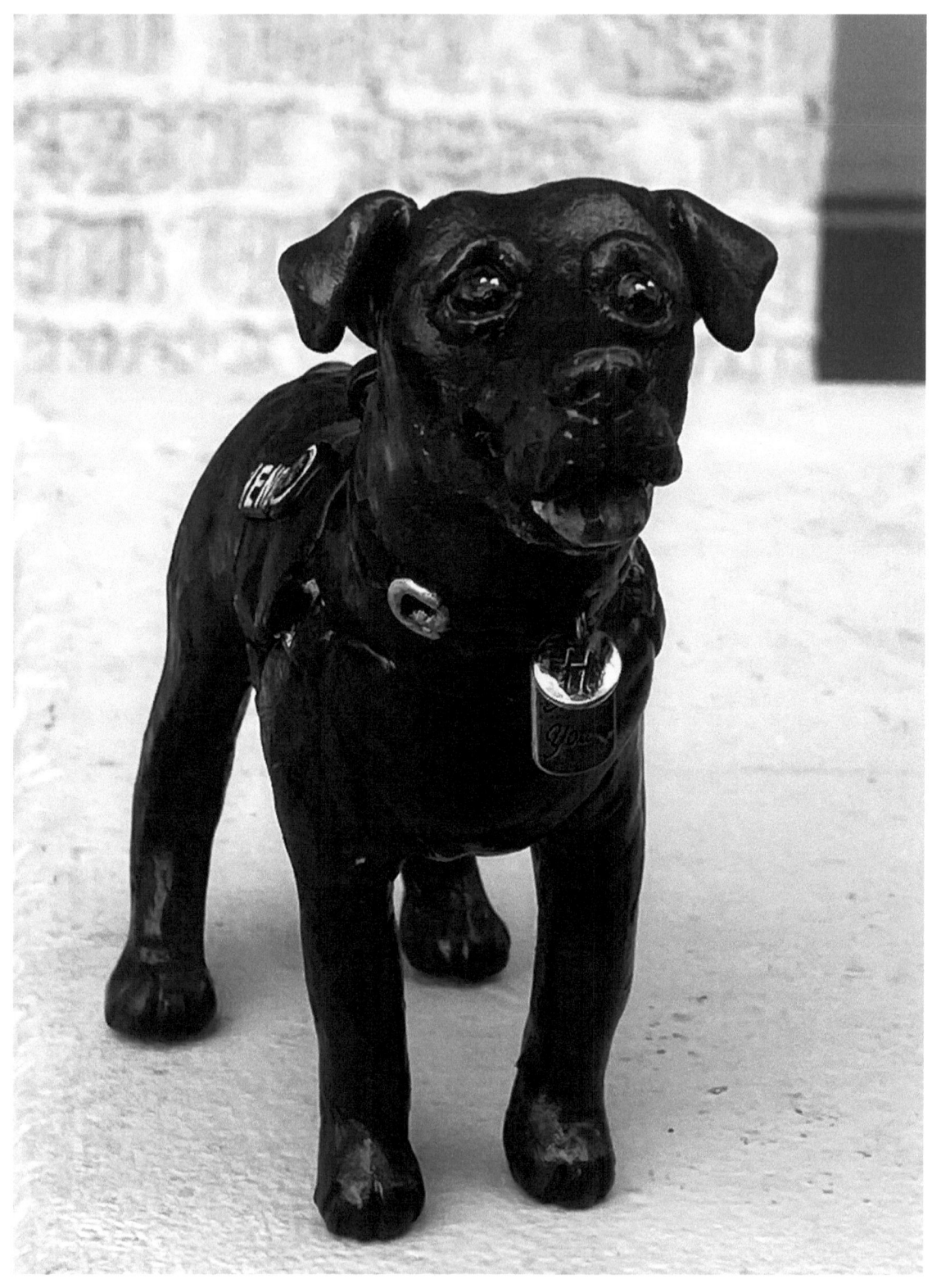

Henry now retired after 13 years of service as an ambassador @fortworthacc

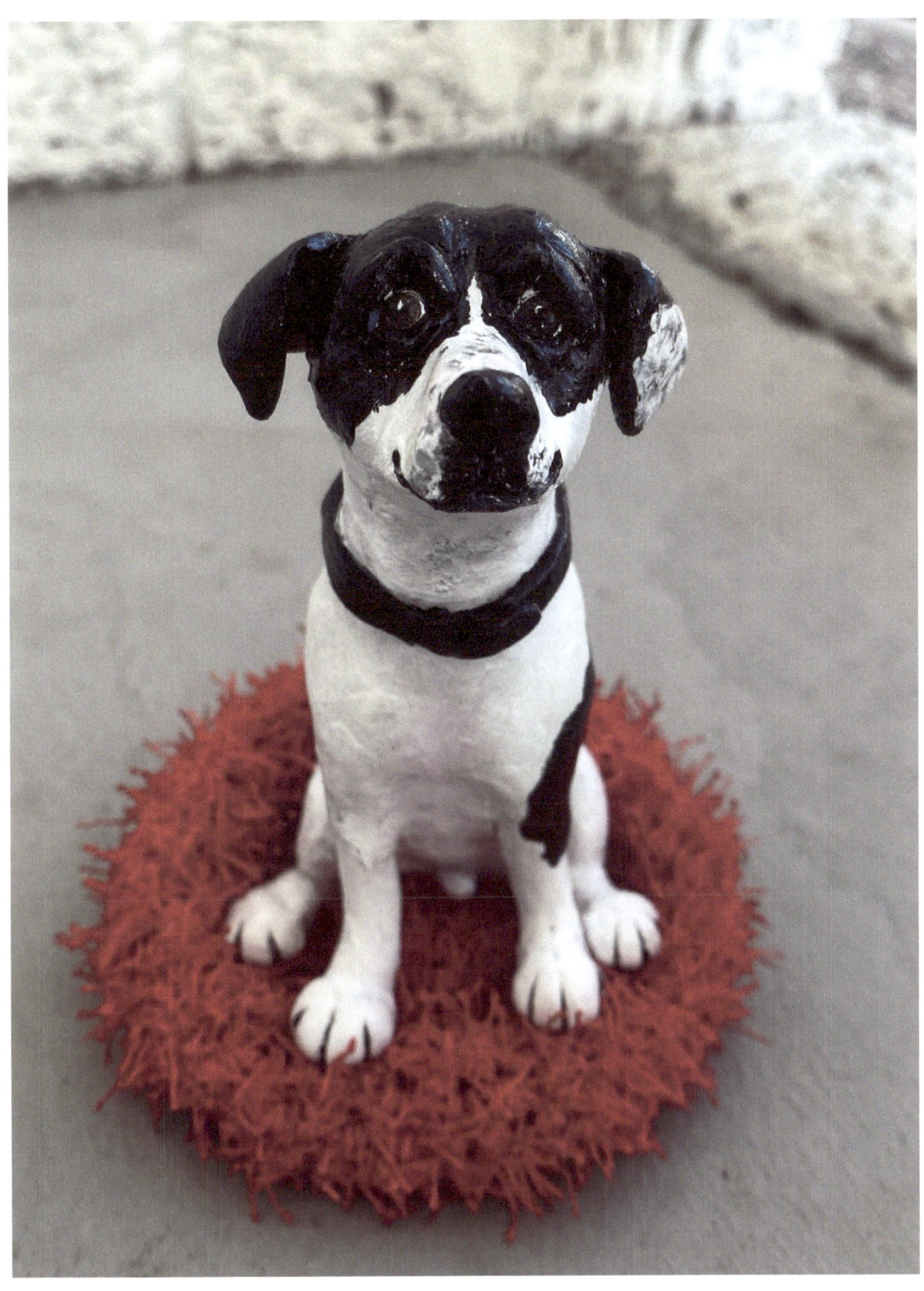

Arthur was a shelter resident @fortworthacc

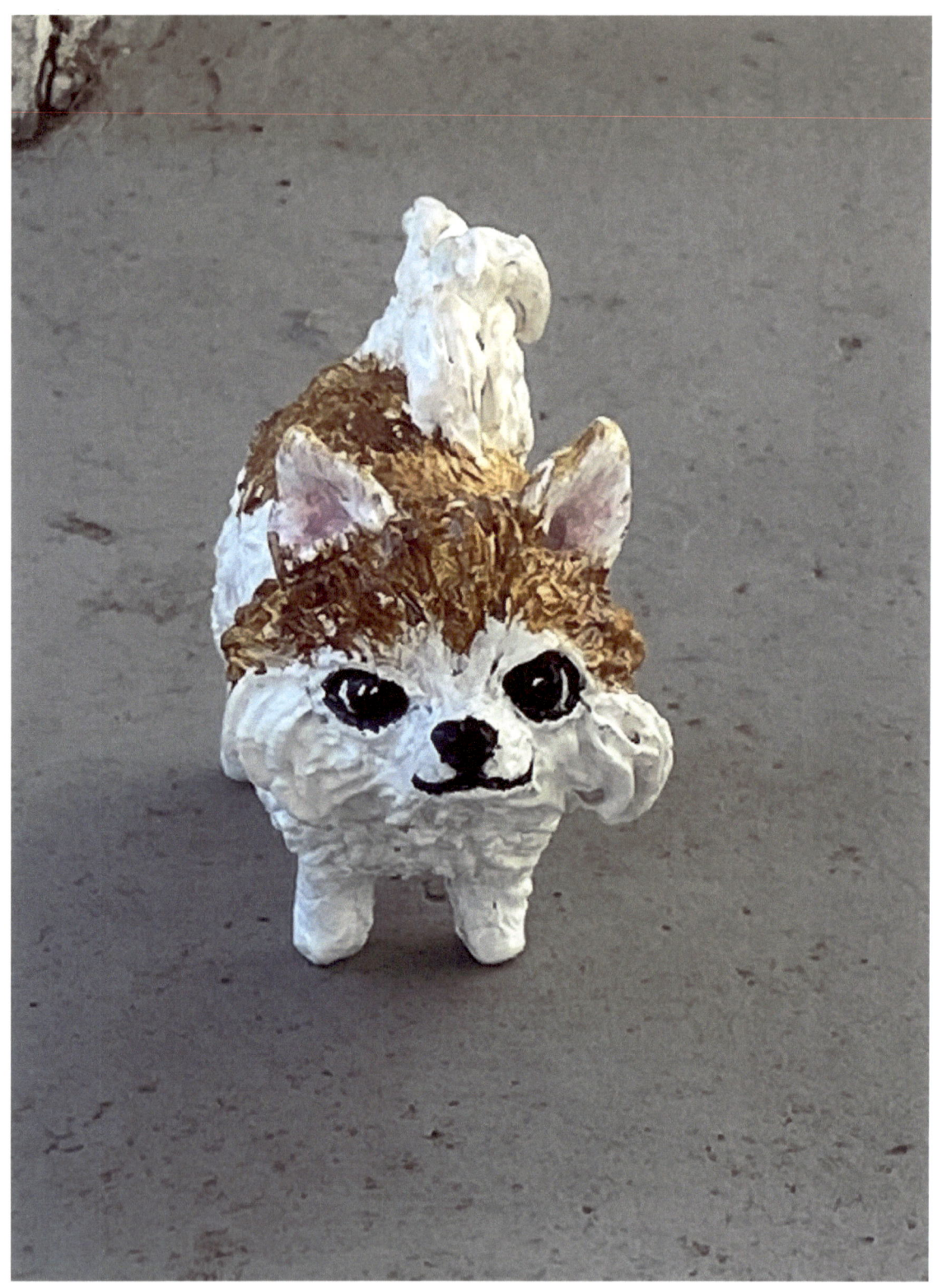

Willow

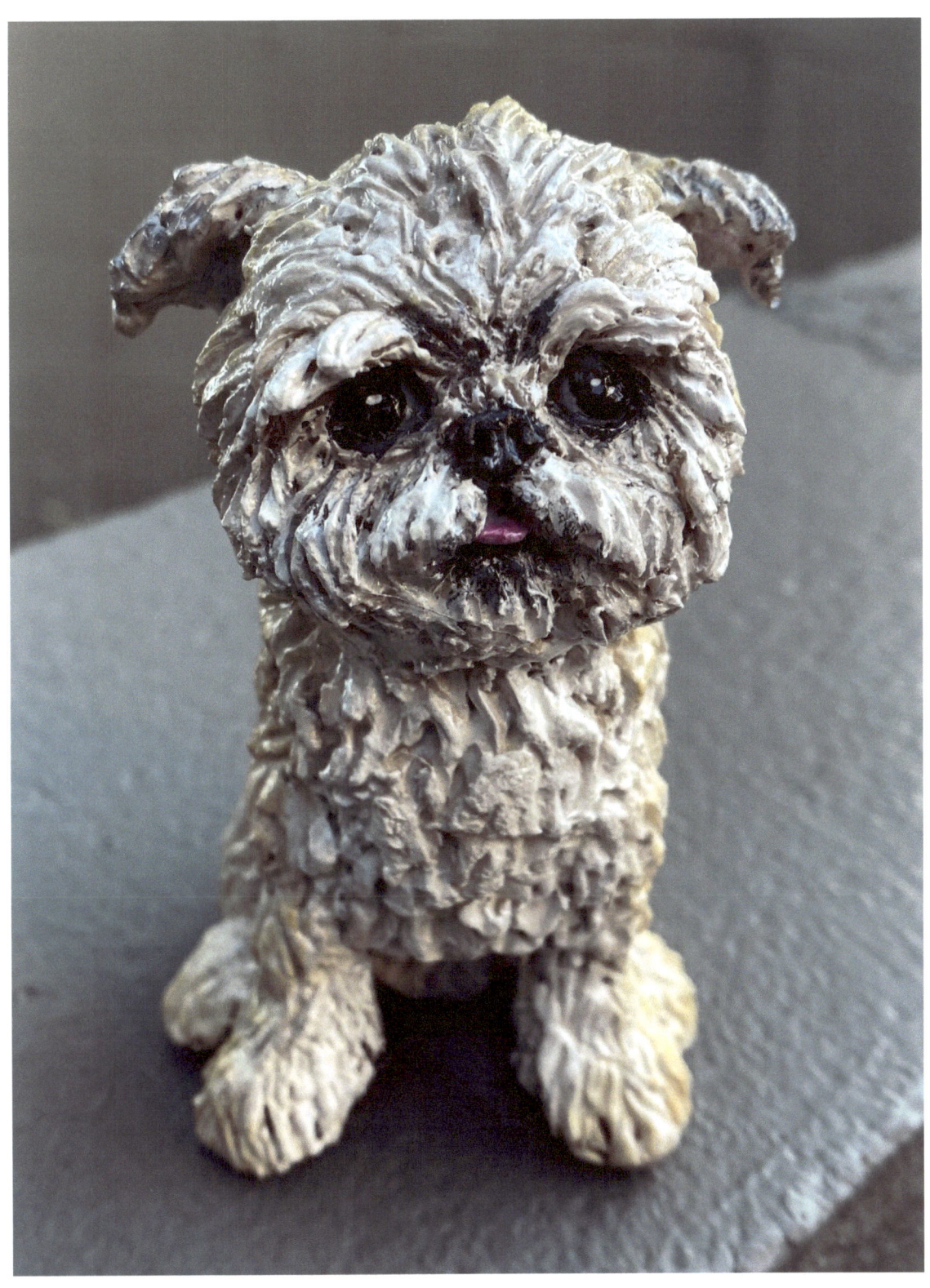

Gilly @monsterandpie

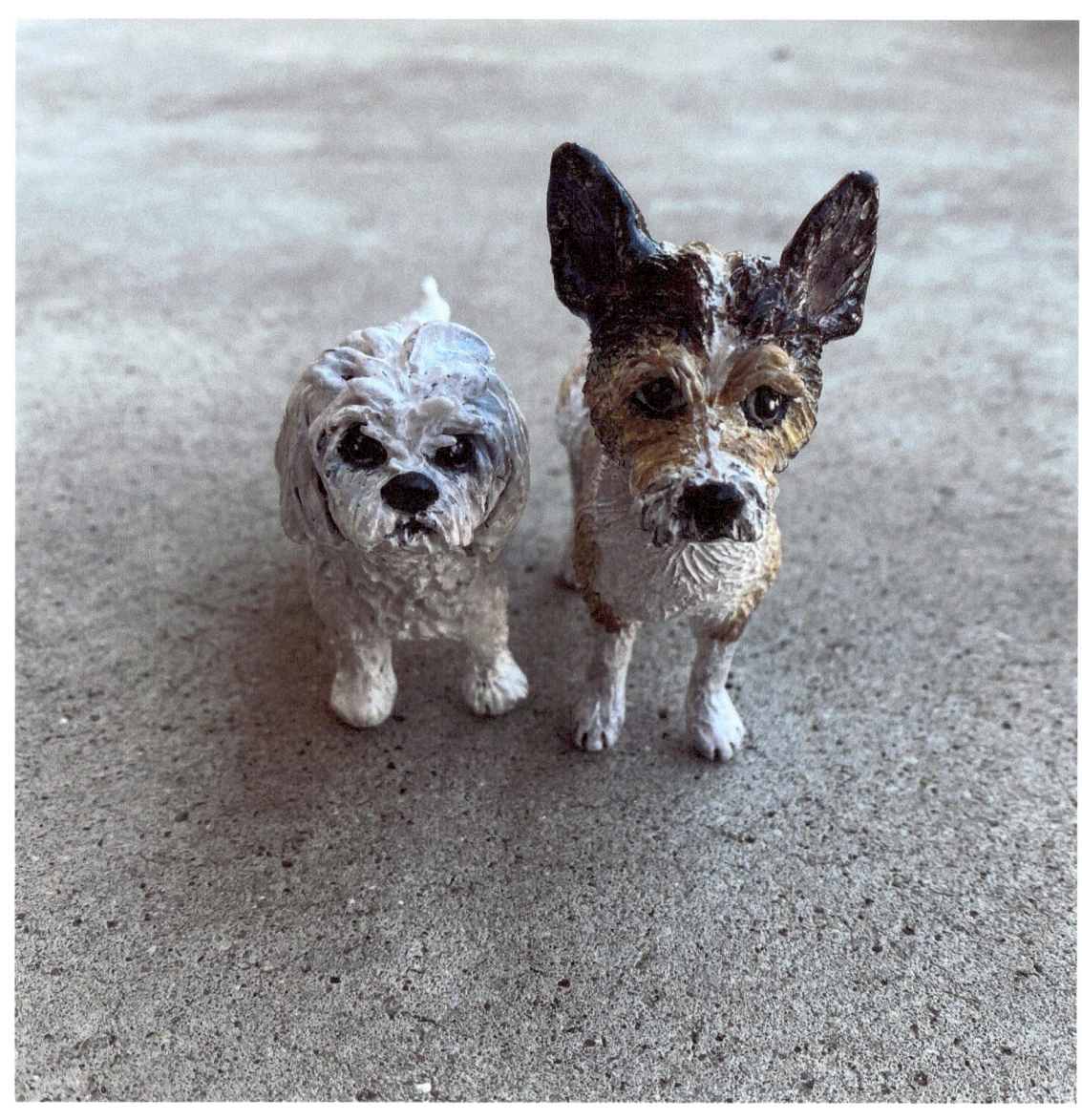

Ginger and Charlie

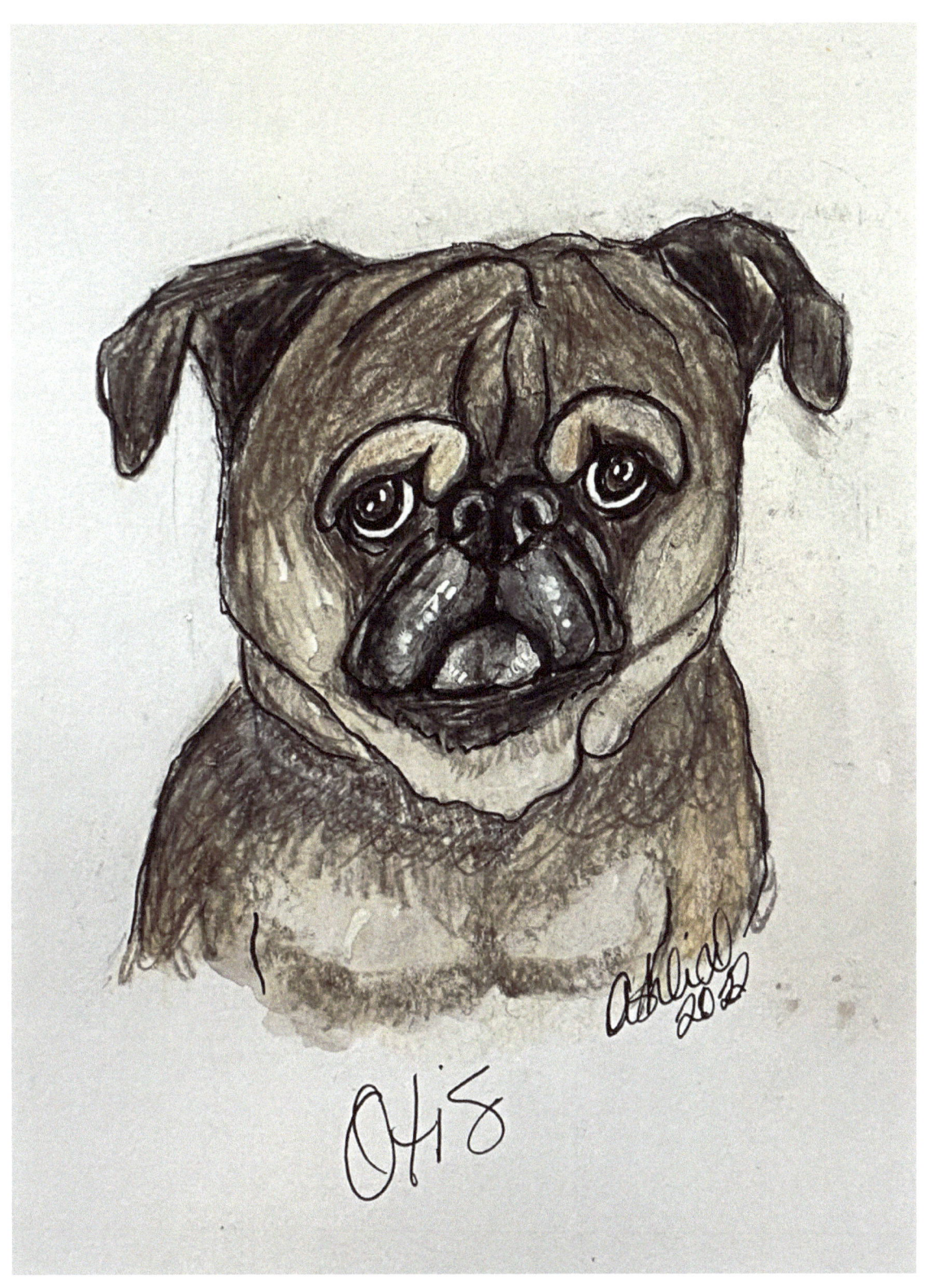

Otis @otisthesnausage

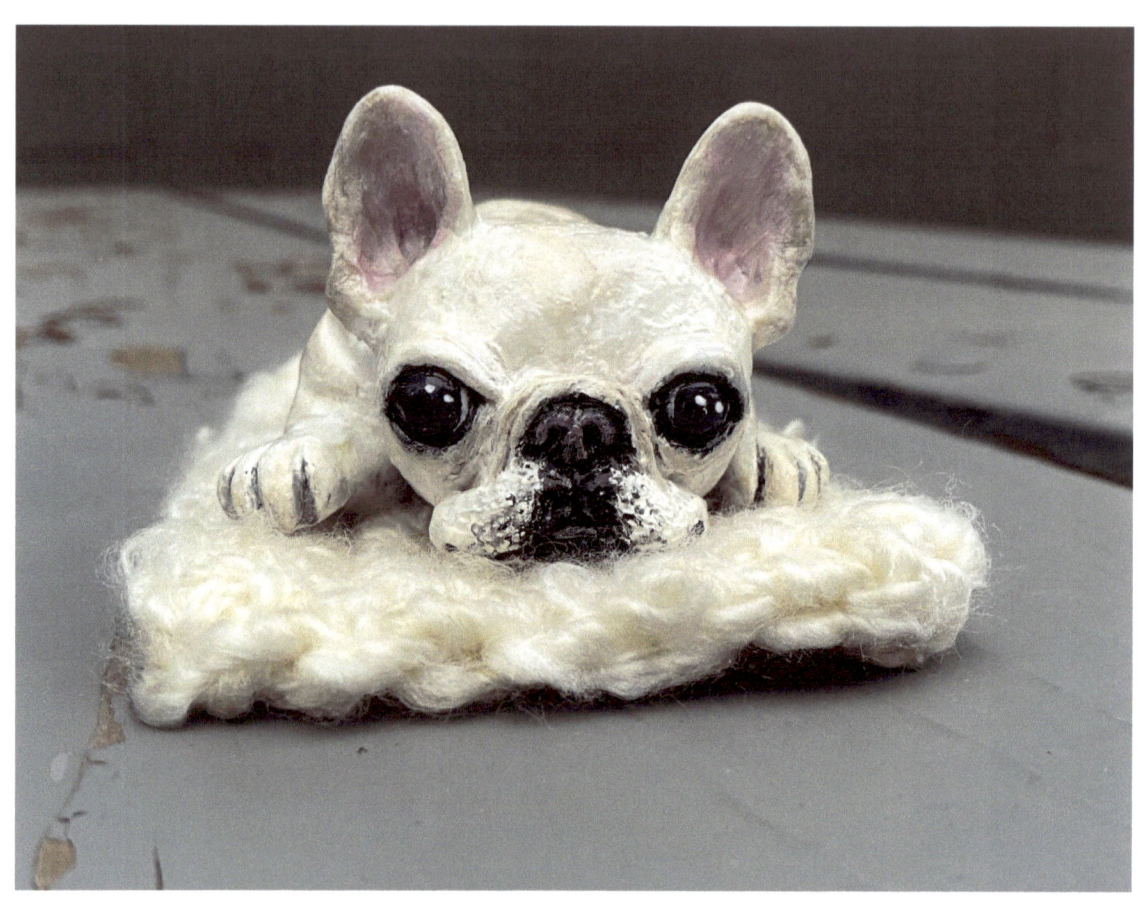

Weston @wtfrenchie

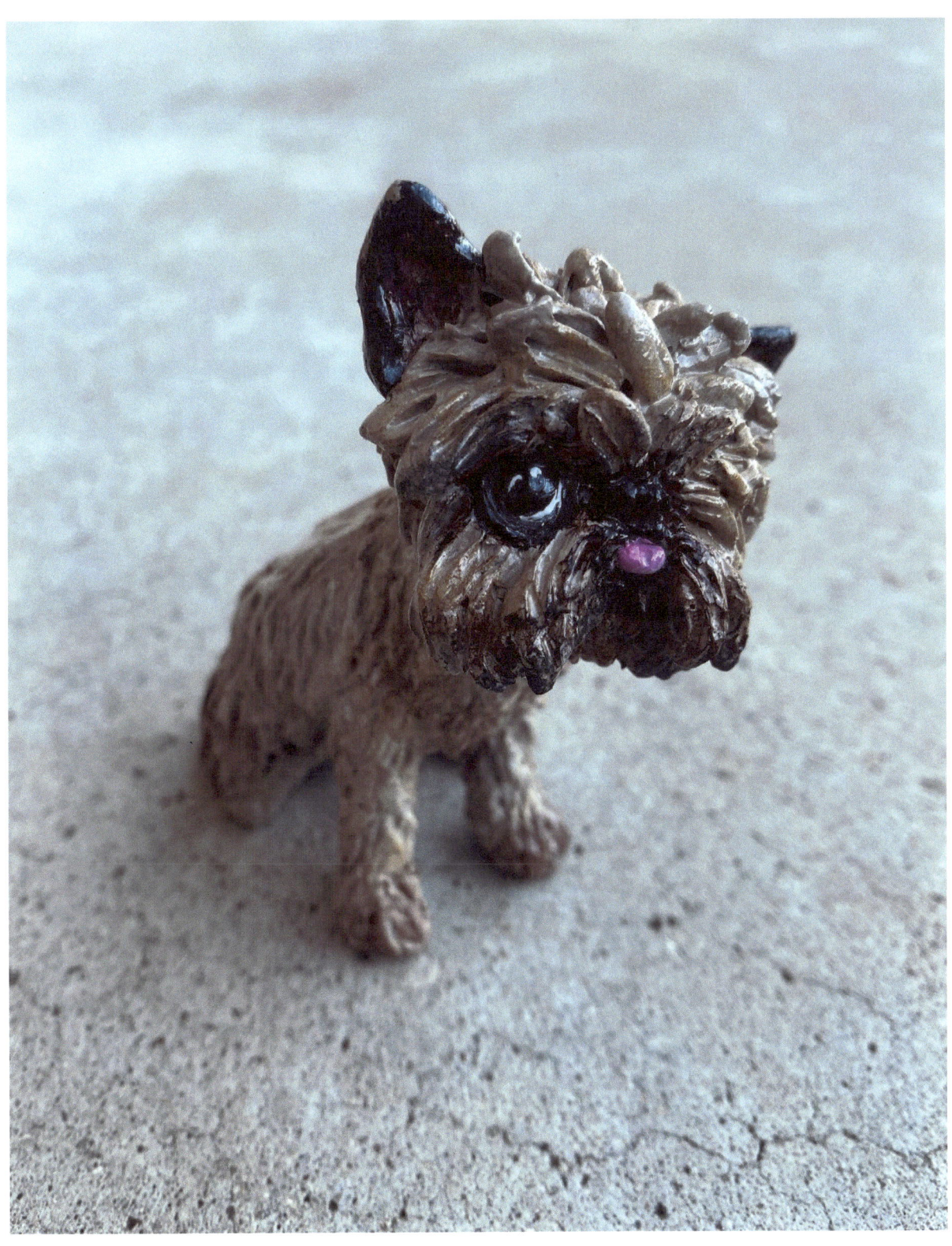

Bean @meeplysparrow

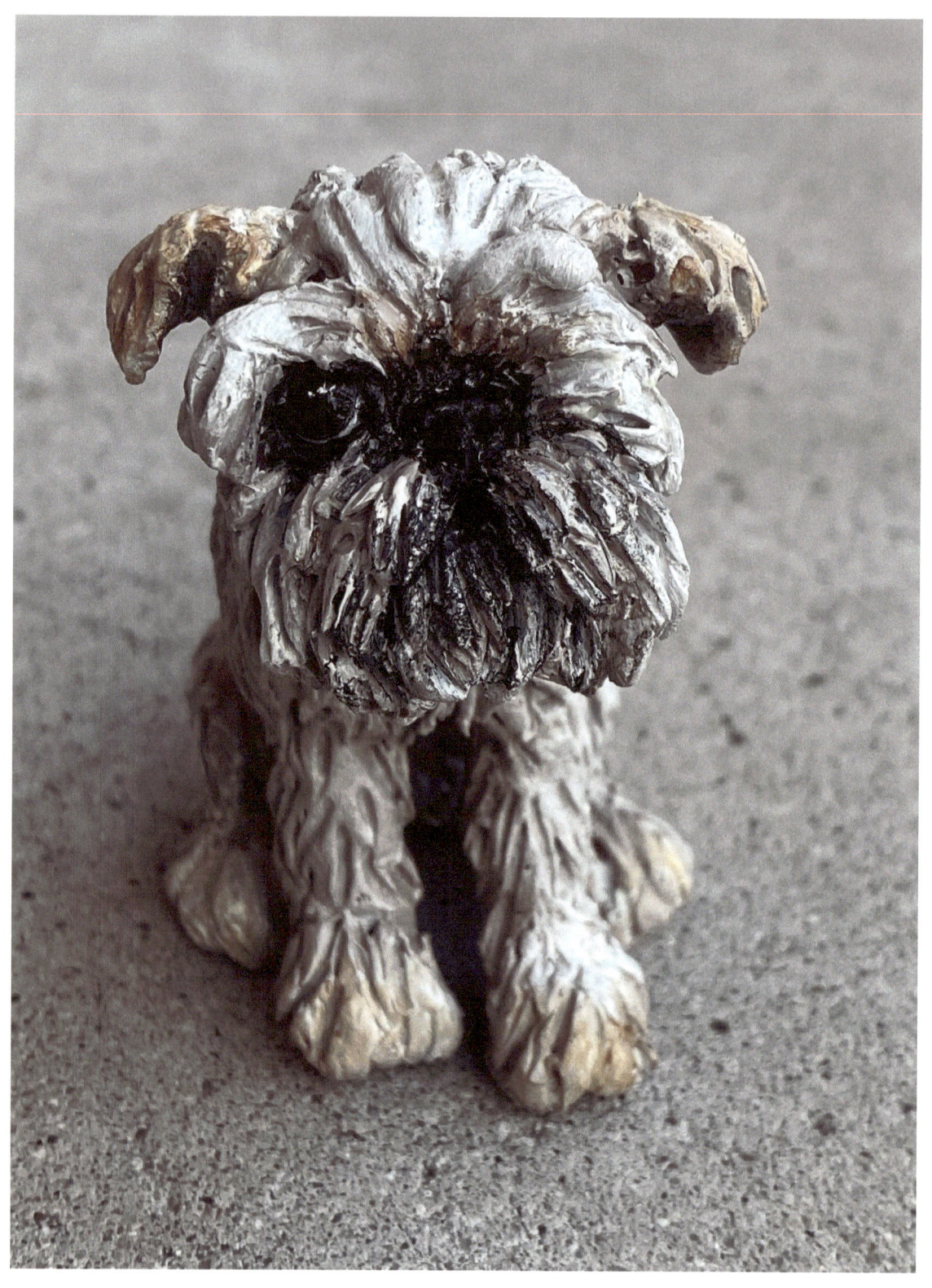

Quincy @monsterandpie

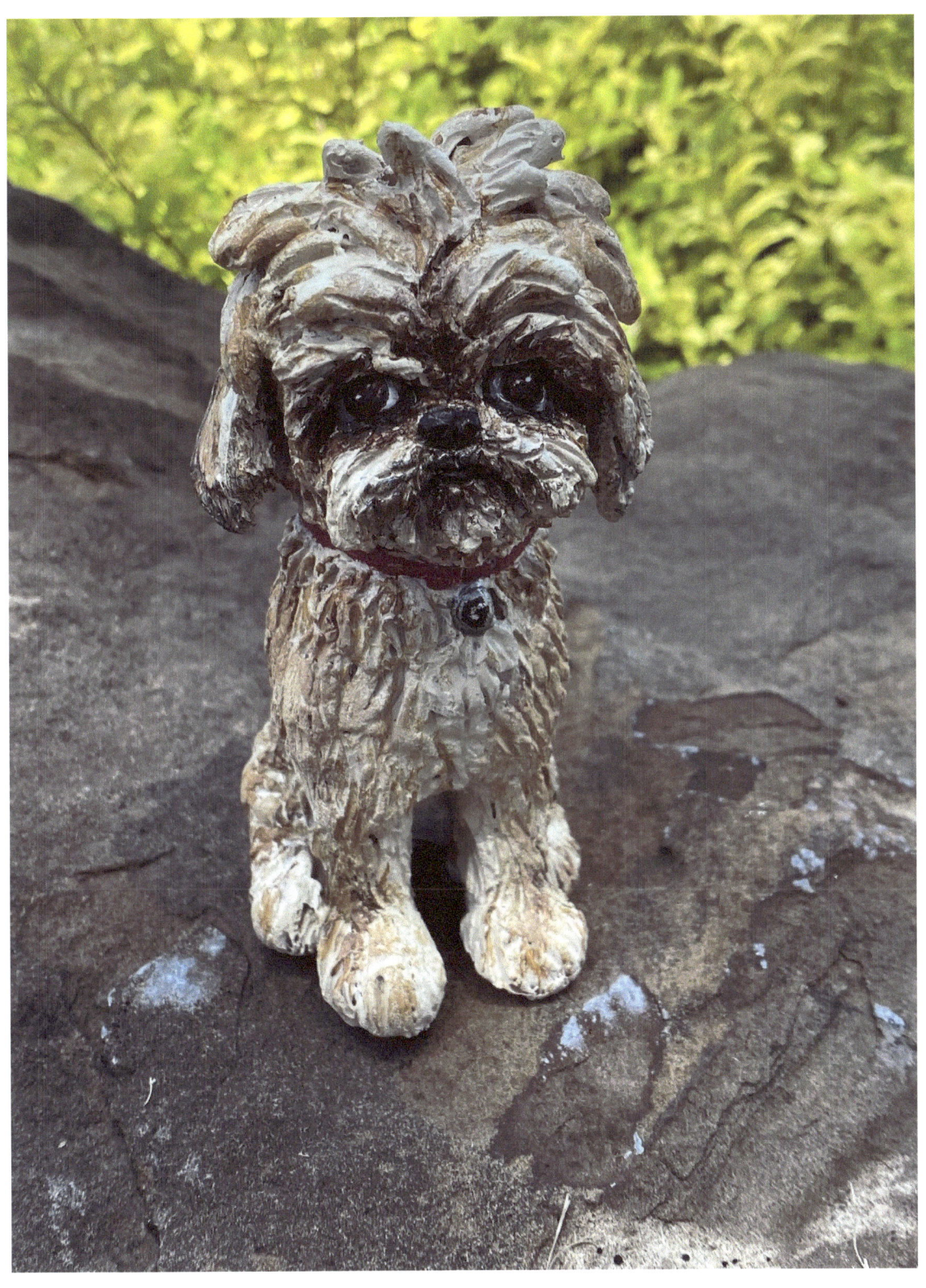

Grimmee @griffongrimmeeandrocki

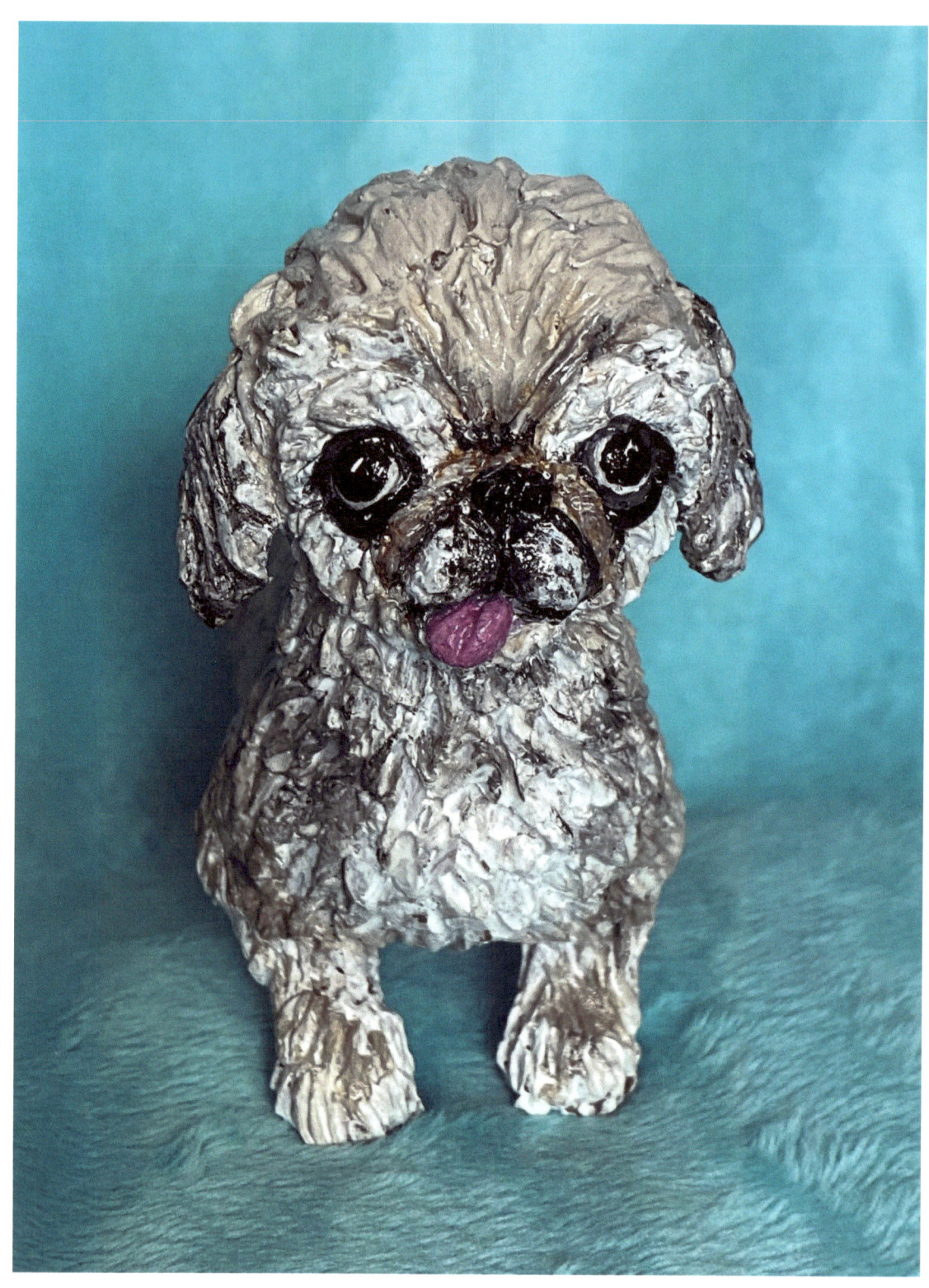

Woof @woofster_the_munchkin

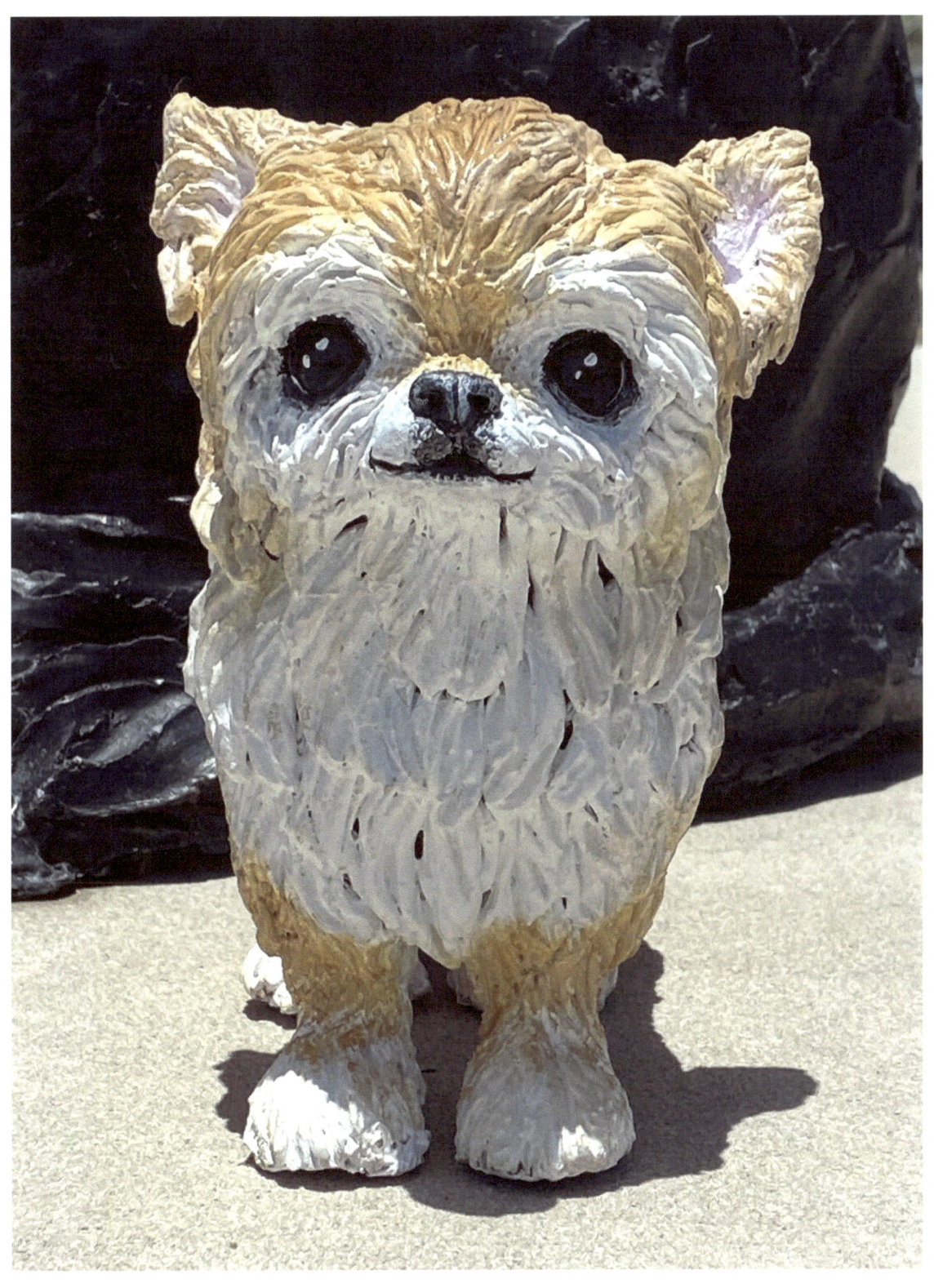

Mr. Hudson @hudsyboo

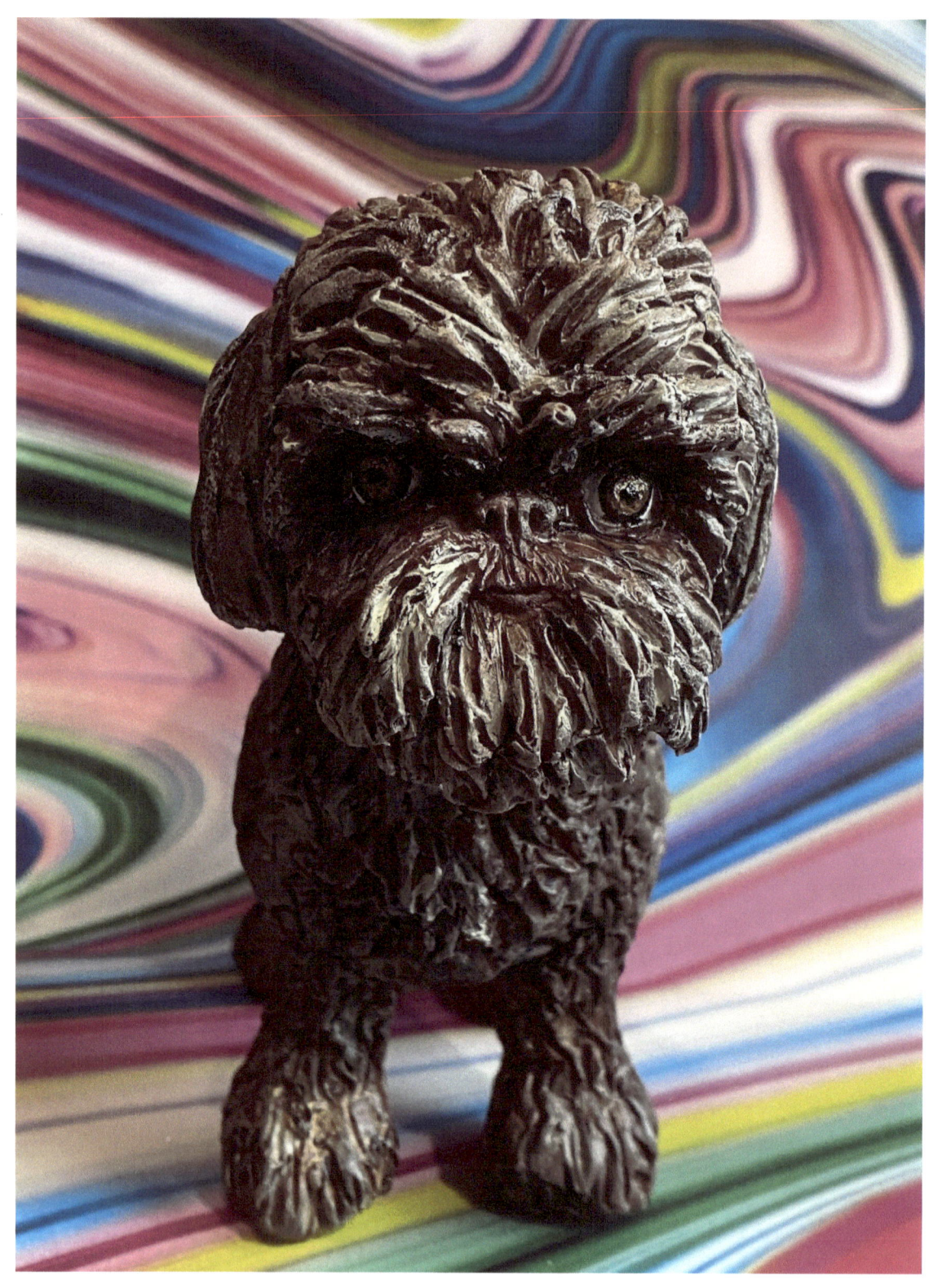

Riley @riley_living.the.life

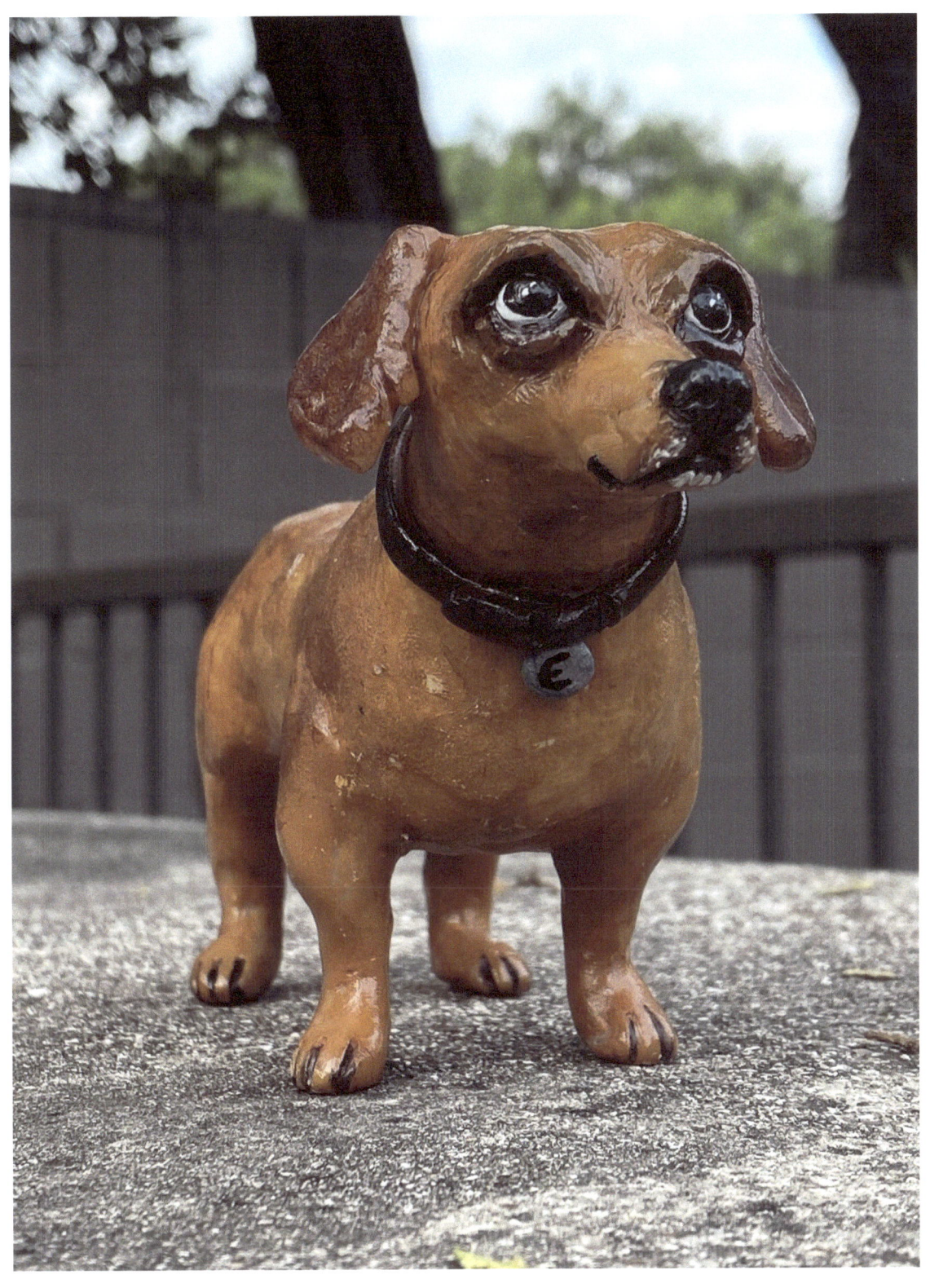

Edgar @edgar_the_weiner

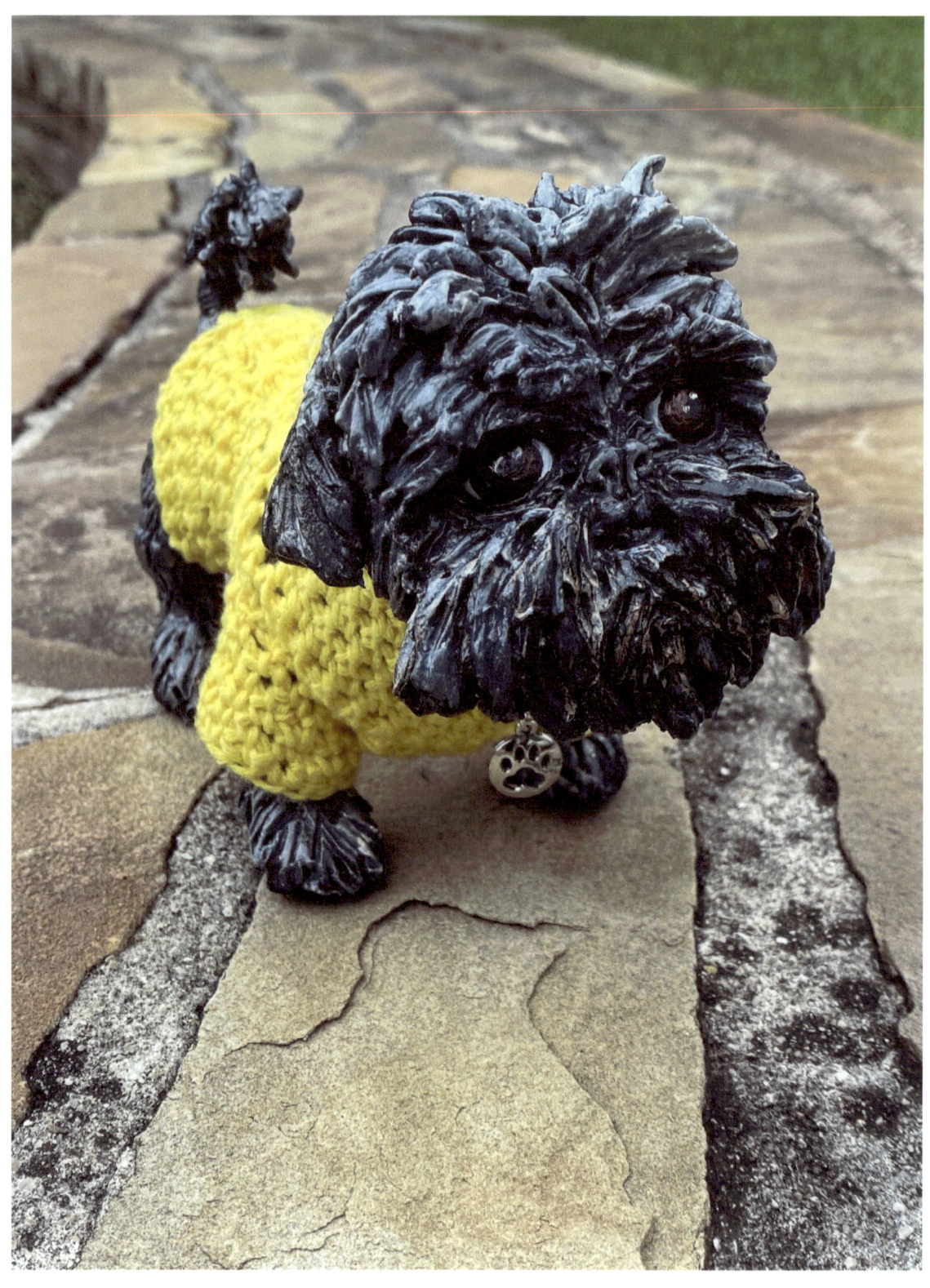

Vivienne Westwoof @youthoughtron

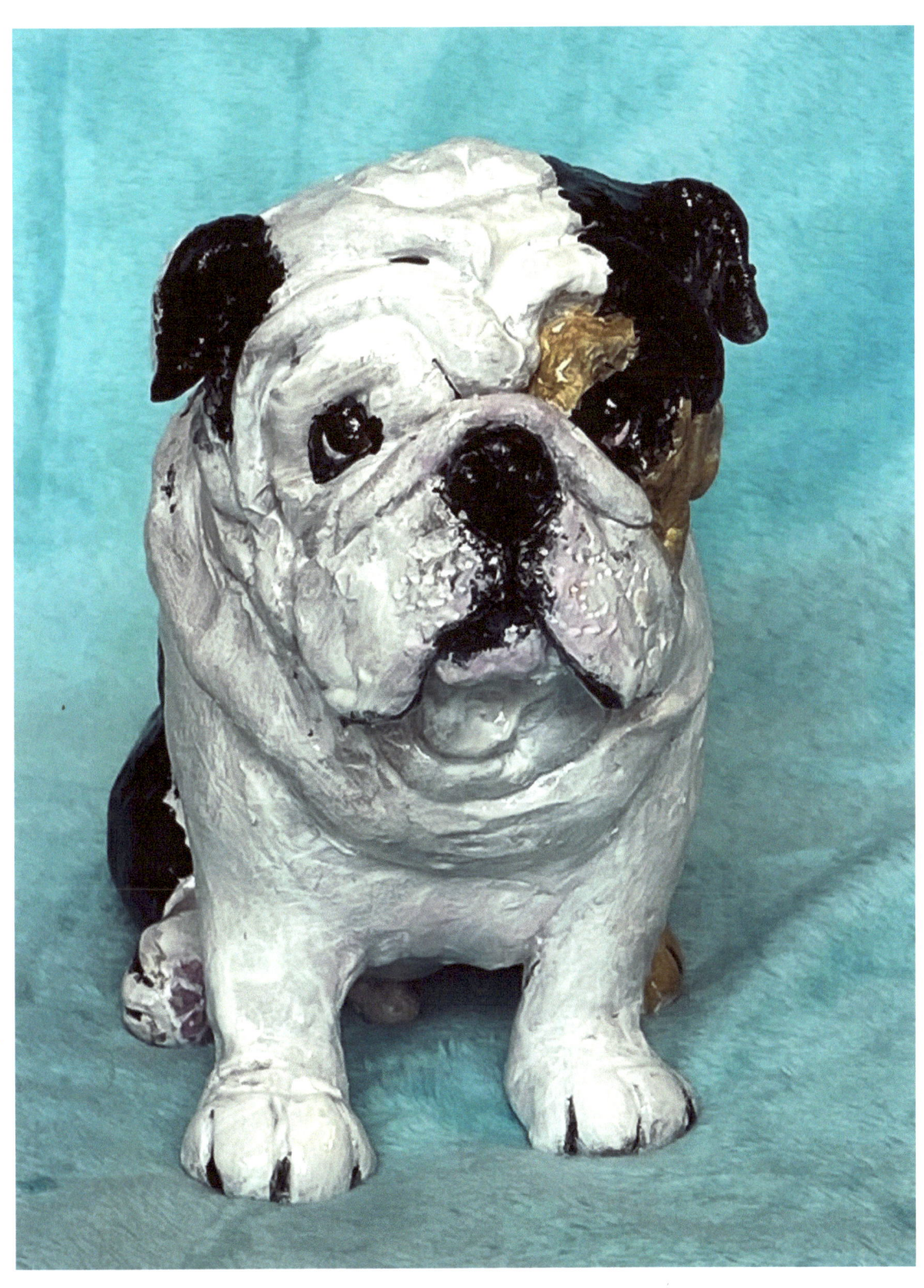

Oso @cars_and_pets

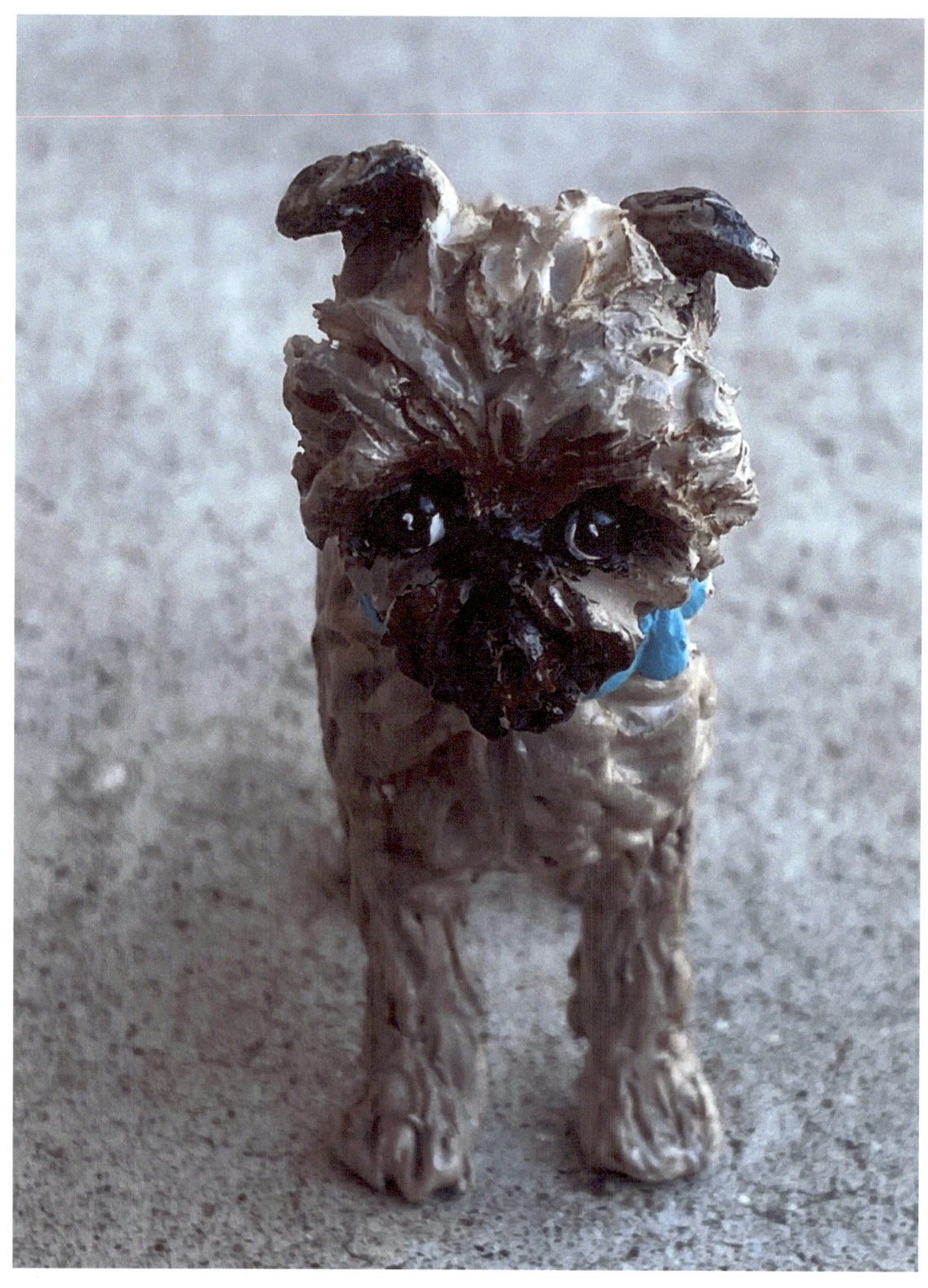

Zippy @zippideedoodog

Contact:

for dog sculptures

https://www.instagram.com/ashlidcartoondogs

ashlidcartoondogs@gmail.com

for drawings

https://www.instagram.com/wagsweekly

https://www.instagram.com/drawmemsashli

for people sculptures (I do not take commissions for people sculptures.)

https://www.instagram.com/rufflittlesculptsbyashli

Etsy shop

https://www.etsy.com/shop/MUTTable

Books available on Amazon:

Ashli D. Wells: cartoon sculptor/poet

Ashli D's Cartoon Dogs: Volume I

Wee M.E. by Ashli D.: using my inside voice

Ashli D's Big Book of Poetry: washing machine dreams

M.E. Best: Starting Over at 50 years

Wags Weekly: Book One

MUTTable: Book One

MUTTable: Book Two

Buy me a Coffee:

https://www.buymeacoffee.com/ashlidwells